The Inward Journey

BOOKS

By
Gene Edwards

Revolution—The Story of the Early Church

A Tale of Three Kings

The Divine Romance

The Prisoner in the Third Cell

The Birth

In the Face of a Church Split (Our Mission)

Preventing a Church Split

Letters to a Devastated Christian

The Inward Journey

The Highest Life

The Secret to the Christian Life

Dear Lillian

The Inward Journey

by Gene Edwards

The SeedSowers

Beaumont, Texas

Dedication

During the six formative and crucial years that Helen and I lived in Tyler, Texas, she was Helen's closest and dearest Christian friend. With her warm heart, wise counsel and ready wit, we both recall her as one of the most remarkable and beautiful among women.

To my dear friend,

Billie Marie

Acknowledgement

To Carman who paid the price of taking the first draft of this book from a yellow note pad covered with my indecipherable scrawl and putting it into typewritten form. To Sandy who came to my rescue and did the final draft. To Brad who did the graphic art. To Annie who played a double role in the production of this book, doing a large part of the retyping *and* the typesetting. And to Kathy who did all of the above plus everything else, which turned out to be the major part of the task. To all of them for engaging in that mysterious art and deep science—far beyond my poor power to comprehend—of finding and correcting misspelled words!

Introduction

The reason for this book finds its genesis in an incident that happened to me shortly after I was converted to Christ.

At the time of my conversion I was a student at East Texas State University in Commerce, Texas. I became a member of the First Baptist Church in that city and also joined the Baptist student fellowship near campus. The summer after my conversion the Lord came and visited that group of about 20 college kids; it was a time so glorious that even now—30 years later—the remembrance of it still brings chills and tears. That visitation lasted about three months, with an afterglow that lasted about a year. As a group we were drawn very close to one another and consequently, as much as possible, did everything together. One thing we did that summer was to pile in a bus and travel out into the unknown, all the way to a conference for young people at the Ridgecrest Baptist Assembly grounds in North Carolina.

I was a rather naive college senior and a very ignorant new Christian when I wandered into the Baptist bookstore located on those grounds. As I entered the store I was absolutely awed by the endless, infinite array of books and the myriad categories they were divided into. Dazed, I walked over to the clerk behind one of the counters and asked, "Where do you keep the books for new Christians?" She looked at me rather puzzled, weighed my question, and replied, "Well, there's no such section." Then she asked, "What is it you're interested in?" That still ranks as one of the most incongruous questions ever asked me. I didn't have the slightest idea what there was to be interested in.

When I left that conference I returned to college, entered the ministry and went on to enroll in the seminary where, for nearly four years, I guess I attempted to read the entire contents of one of the world's largest theological libraries.

Three decades have now passed. I suppose during those years I have read about as many books as a man can afford to buy, borrow or copy. And during those passing years most of my ministry has been spent with college age young people, on four continents and about 30 nations. Wherever I go I am still constantly on the lookout for, please, just one more good book to read. I have found very, *very* few books worth reading in the last 10 years. And every time a new Christian asks me, "What are some good books for me to read," I still draw only a blank and realize that these young people are no better off in their quest than I was when I asked that question so long ago.

Unfortunately, we older Christians fare only a little better. I recall once wanting to learn all I could about the book of Galatians. I ordered every book in print I could find. Then I plowed in. Those books were either drier than Sinai, deader than Adam, more boring than a Sunday morning church service (excuse me, dear reader, but even as a minister of the gospel I have to confess I have never found anything more boring in all of life than sitting in a pew on Sunday morning), or as incomprehensible as Einstein's theory of relativity. This, unfortunately, is the typical book menu from which we "mature" Christians must dine.

Until this day I still pick up literature marked "for the new Christian" and with great disappointment find it either inane, useless, traditional, cranial, old, shallow, irrelevant or carrying within its covers the curse of scholarship. That question still haunts me, "Where *are* the books for new Christians?"

It is with the issuing of this volume that I propose to begin answering that question. If God grants me the grace I intend to write a series of books aimed at college age young people (18-24) new to the faith; books which cover the basics, which lay a solid foundation for a deeper Christian life. Furthermore, I am prepared to break every rule known to literature—be it sacred or secular—to make those books both interesting and easy to read.

If I succeed in the goal set, then these books will not only well serve the new convert but perhaps will speak with profundity even to the mature believer.

The subject covered herein? You might call it a *tour guide*, one that describes what a young believer might expect to encounter experientially on his way down the road toward transformation.

Gene Edwards
Quebec City,
Canada

Chris Young
Portland, Maine

Bill Young
Wales, Great Britain

Dear Uncle Bill,

You've heard by now of my turn-around in life. I really did have a rather overwhelming experience with the Lord. But that was several months ago. I'm sorry I haven't written to tell you.

Let me get to the point. I'm not going to ask you, "Why do men suffer?" or "Why does a loving God allow pain in His creation?" Now I might have asked that last week, but I'm a little better off this week!

Uncle Bill, the truth is, I'm having my first encounter with His chisel after months of knowing His peace, love and joy. I'd like to ask you, if you will, to set down in straightforward words just what part suffering will play in my life for the next forty or fifty years. That's all. But if you throw in a few "why's" I assure you I won't be offended!

Your nephew and your brother,
Chris

Bill Young
Wales, Great Britain

Chris Young
Portland, Maine

Dear Chris:

Yes, your mother wrote me and told me of your having received the Lord's life. Wonderful! As far as writing you, you caught me at a perfect time. I'm sick in bed! I may be here for weeks. In fact, I may eventually have to be operated on.

Chris, here's what I'll try to do—between grunts and groans I'll be scribbling notes to you. From time to time I'll gather up and send a stack of them to you. I hope to be working on a manuscript on the subject of suffering, but I doubt it will be finished for years; nonetheless, if I can get some of it in shape, I may send a draft of it to you. But for right now the manuscript needs a great deal of work, so give me some time on that possibility. I will begin the letters immediately.

Enjoy the Lord. Those first couple of years as a Christian are some of the most memorable of life.

Your brother in Christ,
Uncle Bill

Part I

Chapter 1

Chris Young had been a Christian for only a very short time . . . and he was very sad. Tears flowed freely and sobs were deep. He sat on his bed, his head whirling with questions.

The dorm room was small, the hall unusually quiet, even for a Sunday evening. Chris buried his face in his hands and sobbed uncontrollably, sure no one was around to hear. Eventually he grew quiet, his body too tired to cry any longer. For a long while he sat silent until the very eeriness of the silence began to bother him. Suddenly Chris realized he didn't want to open his eyes. He was afraid to—he had the overwhelming sense that his bed was resting on the edge of some sort of chasm . . . and that someone was standing in the room. Somehow Chris knew what he would see when he opened his eyes. The room had dissolved, he was sure of that . . . and if he did open his eyes he would be staring straight into timelessness. Without opening his eyes, Chris raised his head.

"Where am I, and who are you?"

"Come," answered a quiet, level voice. "Come, I will answer your questions . . . as they can be answered."

Chris threw back the covers and finally dared crack open his eyes. The universe was gone; creation and every atom in it . . . was not. His eyes still not fully open, the young Christian ventured again, "Where are we?"

"Before."

"Before?"

"Before all things. Before everything. Before anything. Before nothingness."

With that, Christian Young opened his eyes. The bed was gone. Someone stood behind him. Before him was neither day nor night, time nor space. Before him was an absence of all things. Chris turned, then, to see a creature not too much unlike a man, yet surely not a man. Chris was about to ask the obvious, but the answer came sooner than the question.

"I am Messenger. Come."

"Please, where are we?" said the young man again, sure that on this try he would receive a reply.

Messenger was robed in something white that radiated a soft light, his form only partially discernible within the glow; nonetheless, Chris could see that his hand was raised and he was pointing.

"That way. We shall travel that way," he said as they began moving into the non-darkness that stretched before them. "We are all that there is. Neither time, eternity, nor creation has yet begun. Yet, even we are but guests here, and that only for the moment."

Chris did not speak, but he did follow. Neither words nor thoughts seemed appropriate as the two moved through this strange progenitor of darkness.

"What is that light ahead?" came the startled words of Christian, for it seemed nothing could exist here.

"You have asked, 'Why all this pain? What is its purpose? Why is it allowed?' " said Messenger, turning full round to face the young man. Uneasy and quite unsure of himself, as though he had caused some major problem with his question, Chris stumbled a reply.

"Yes, but they aren't entirely my questions. I'm

taking this class . . . and . . ." Christian stopped speaking; such words seemed absurd here. "I am confused, though," he added more realistically.

"Then let us move toward that light. There you will find an answer. Perhaps it will *not* be the answer to your . . . or *their* . . . questions. But you will find . . ." Messenger paused and looked intently into young Christian's eyes. "We are at the edge. We are very nearby to beginning."

"Is that light . . . uh . . . beginning?"

"No. That is something before the beginning. Before angels, before the heavenlies, before all realms. Before man, earth, skies, time and space. Before all. All, except suffering and pain."

"*They* are here? Before anything?"

"Before *anything*," said Messenger, his voice fading.

Messenger's steps had become slow and unsure. Just in front of them was a light, something like a street lamp might make.

"You may go alone. I have no desire to see what is there . . . not twice," said Messenger in a voice almost cold.

"Just beyond the light, there is something else out there. Isn't there a boundary?" Chris asked.

"No," replied Messenger. "There is nothing else, nor can there be, until there is first *that* . . ." Messenger pointed again in the direction of the light. "*That* must be before all things. That and pain, *that* and suffering were before even the beginnings . . . nor could there have been anything . . . unless . . ." Messenger fell silent.

Cautiously, Christian moved forward. Plainly, there was something lying out there before him.

"Oh, no. Oh, no. No," cried Christian. "No, no, please, no!" he cried again as he dropped to his knees.

Just before him, lying in a pool of blood, lay the cold, dead, and mangled form of a snow-white lamb.

For

> He was slain
> *Before* the foundation
> Of the world.

Chapter 2

"This is a very hot place," said Christian wearily.

"You are in southeast Palestine."

"That's a city over there, isn't it?"

"Yes, but we need not enter it for our purposes. That pile of dung over there is our destination."

"A pile of dung! Where have I heard of that before?" Christian thought for a moment, then exclaimed, "A pile of dung! Job. Will I see Job?"

Messenger did not reply, but moved steadily toward the heap of stench. Finally, he spoke again. "It is to this place that things dead are carried."

"Will they bring Job out here? But he wasn't dead."

"But as good as dead," came Messenger's sober reply. "But no, you'll not see Job sitting on this pile. That is all past. Job is well and he has been fully restored to health and wealth."

Christian stood transfixed for a moment. There was something in that bit of news that was of tremendous importance and he was seeking to comprehend it. Slowly he spoke. "If I could meet Job, a *restored* Job, I could speak to perhaps the one man in history who could explain the significance of suffering . . . at least *his*!"

Messenger ignored Christian's words, continuing only to stare at the dung heap. Christian moved to his side and joined in staring.

"What an awful place to be dumped," Christian observed, finally. Then, feeling that statement was not quite an adequate expression of his feelings, he shook his head and said, "No wonder we speak of the patience of Job."

"The patience of whom . . . ?" came a voice from behind.

"Of Job," Christian said spontaneously as he turned. "And who are you?" he added.

"Job. None other. And whoever said I had patience?" he asked with a laugh. "Job, the world's greatest griper, is more to the truth."

"You're Job? But you're too young to be Job!"

"Ah, if you would also include Mrs. Job in that assessment, we would both thank you!"

"Did you *really* live on that . . . dung heap?"

"Ah, yes," said Job with a sweep of his hand as he moved briskly toward the dung heap. "Allow me to show you my second home. Not nearly as nice as was the first."

With that, Job stormed up the dung hill with Christian in an unsteady pursuit.

"What did you learn about suffering while you . . . lived here?" asked Christian.

Obviously surprised that anyone would be interested, Job looked intently at the young man for a long time.

"Crocodiles. That's what I learned. Crocodiles!"

"Huh?" said Christian, looking for a moment very much like a little boy.

"Crocodiles. The Lord God created crocodiles. I didn't. To add insult, He created the crocodile before He created me. Nor did He find the least problem in creating it without consulting me on either its design, purpose, or its color. In fact, He has yet to explain to me why He dared create such a monstrosity...or

20

what purpose the beastly thing is supposed to serve . . . None at all, is my guess!''

"What have crocodiles got to do with your . . . losing everything on earth . . . and ending up here?''

"Nothing. Absolutely nothing. Except this: It appears that our Lord views the creating of crocodiles and the decreeing of human disasters with about the same disdain for outside advice . . . and with as little explanation I might add!''

Softening a little from the boisterous role which he was obviously enjoying, Job lowered his voice.

"Son," he continued, "it appears we have a God who has supreme confidence in His own judgment. Nor can He be persuaded to show a great deal of interest in explaining Himself. He keeps His counsel to Himself, it appears; nor is He perturbed in the least that we're perturbed about His not being perturbed.''

"Is *that* all you learned? I mean, after all you went through.''

"That's all," said Job with finality . . . and began walking away.

"Nothing else?" called out Christian.

"No," replied Job without turning. "But," said he, raising his index finger in a gesture of discovery, "I didn't need to learn anything else. I saw Him. Getting questions answered seems rather a paltry thing in comparison to having *seen* Him.''

Job walked on. Christian knew that he would hear no more on that matter, at least not from Job. But to Christian's surprise, Job turned again and called out.

"I simply cannot wait to tell my wife about your jest of me, she'll love it. So will my friends. 'The patience of Job' '' . . . his voice trailed off in laughter.

Christian stood there for a long time. "Gee, it's hard to realize that that was the man Satan went after with such a vengeance!"

"Shhh," said Messenger. "He knows nothing of that!"

"He doesn't?" said Christian, wide-eyed. "You mean . . . *nothing*!?"

"Nothing," replied Messenger. "A great deal of life's tragedies . . . and joys . . . have their origin—and explanation—in places unseen."

"And for reasons unknown," murmured Christian.

Chapter 3

"It will be better that you not inquire concerning this man's name, not in the beginning. Just visit with him a moment, that should suffice," said Messenger as they approached a large black tent that seemed to be weighted down by the sweltering heat.

The tent flap was open and Christian was eager to get out of the sun's blast.

"Hello," said Christian rather slowly as he observed the old man sitting before him.

"Be seated," returned an ancient voice.

The two sat in silence for a long time. Uncomfortable with the silence, Christian finally observed, "I'm not sure exactly why I'm here."

"Nor am I," said the old man with an ever so slight twinkle in his voice.

"Let's see. Well, sir, have you ever been sick . . . like sitting on a dung hill waiting to die?"

"Can't say that I have," came the response.

"Poor health, maybe?" continued Christian.

"No, never," replied the old man, valiantly trying to be helpful.

"Others in your family?"

"Nooo," sang the old gentleman. "Fact is, everyone in my family tends to live to a terribly old age!"

"Wars, plagues? Anything like that?"

"Much less than most folks I know," came the cheerful reply.

"Tragedy? "

"Tragedy?" said the old man thoughtfully. "I suppose not. No. No great personal tragedies. Oh, I did once work for an awfully ornery uncle. But no tragedies."

Christian sank back feeling utterly defeated. Looking toward the door flap in hopes of getting some signal from Messenger, who—not surprisingly—was nowhere to be seen. Christian decided it was time to depart. Losing Messenger from view was rather unnerving.

Standing to his feet, Christian said numbly, "I think I'd better go."

The old man leaned forward and began struggling to raise himself. A servant entered and assisted him to his feet, revealing a grotesquely gnarled body.

"You're, you're . . ." Christian struggled to find a replacement for the word deformed. "You're lame," he finally exclaimed.

"So I am," said the old man in mock surprise. "So I am!" After a moment of dragging his withered leg across the room, the old man joined the youth at the entrance of the tent. There stood Messenger. For a moment, the eyes of Messenger and the patriarch remained fixed on one another. "You have been to this tent before?" inquired the ancient one.

"On several occasions. Once to visit your grandfather, and . . ."

"Yes, I know. You are Messenger." Then turning to Christian, he said cheerfully, "You are very fortunate. As far as I know, this one doesn't know how to wrestle."

Christian stared first at one, then the other, looking for a clue that would lift his obvious confusion.

"Sir, before I go, your hip: is that a recent thing?"

"Let me think," said the old man, wisely. "No, as I recall that happened to me long ago."

"Farewell, Prince," said Messenger to the ancient one.

"Goodbye," cracked the worn voice of the old man.

"I didn't learn anything," said Christian to Messenger, in a half protest as they walked away. "He's never been sick, or anything like Job. He's just a saintly old man with a broken hip. A . . . a . . . wait a minute," cried Christian as he whirled around. "Sir, how came you by that broken hip?"

"An angel did me the favor," came the old man's delightful response.

Messenger placed his hand upon the shoulder of Christian and whispered, "Suffering, brokenness, pain you will find, come to man in *many* forms."

They walked on a short distance, Christian sensing that Messenger had something else to say.

Finally, still speaking in a whisper, his eyes never moving from a forward gaze, Messenger added . . . almost as to the wind, "It took a lifetime of God at His best to break that man, and even then . . . only when He touched him at the strongest point in his life."

Chapter 4

The stench of the Egyptian dungeon was staggering. Christian braced himself against the slimy wall of the darkened hallway, then pulled back in repulsion. His other hand over his mouth and nose, he stumbled along behind Messenger, passing cell after cell of hideous, unclean creatures some might dare call men. At the end of this eerie dungeon was one last cell.

"Here," said Messenger. "See that man. He is here unjustly."

With almost unbearable will, Christian stared at the sight before him, a filthy, matted mass of humanity.

"Who are you? Why are you here?" asked Christian, keenly aware that the thing before him might not be able to speak. Christian turned to repeat his question to Messenger. "Who is he, Messenger?"

"A future ruler of Egypt, second only to Pharaoh," came the soft words of Messenger, uttered too quietly for the prisoner to hear.

"Then why is he here!?" exclaimed Christian.

There was a groan, followed by labored breathing from the cell's captive.

> They meant it to me for evil.
> But *He* meant it to me for good.

Chapter 5

"Wait here," ordered Messenger.

Christian paused and looked down. They were on a narrow ledge high on a mountainside. A craggy precipice lay just beneath his feet. Sighing, he leaned back and pressed hard against the mountain's side.

"Who goes there?" came a frightened cry.

"A friend," replied the calm voice of Messenger. Christian edged forward, straining to glimpse the mysterious encounter that was taking place a few feet beyond his view. The sight of this meeting would be denied him. Christian could only listen.

"Are you of the king's court?" came the second question.

"None of this earth," was the steady reply of Messenger.

"Then who are you?"

"A friend."

"How did you find me? Do others know of this place?"

"Your secret is ours alone, and will remain so."

"What do you want of me?" came a slightly more confident voice.

"A moment ago as we approached, you were singing?" inquired Messenger of the man squatting in front of a small cave on the side of the mountain ledge.

"Yes, I often do. There is little else I can do."

"But there is surely reason beyond that."

"Things I feel here, deep inside me, I often write them down."

"The content of the goat skin bag beside you, are your writings there?"

"Yes, along with some stale meat."

"May I borrow the sack from you for a moment? I have a young friend with me to whom I desire to show them."

"You are a strange person . . . with a strange request," said the man as he handed the cracked leather sack to Messenger.

"I will return them to you in a moment," said Messenger, as he turned back, effortlessly making his way along the narrow ledge toward Christian.

"I have reason to ask you to look at these," said Messenger as he handed the bag to Christian.

"Here? On this ledge? Now?" came Christian's disbelieving response.

"The man beyond the corner *lives* on this ledge, young Christian. Besides, I doubt you will fall."

"Read," continued Messenger in an unmistakable command.

Christian balanced himself carefully as he squatted precariously before the open bag of scrolls. One by one he opened them and read. At first he read each scroll in its entirety. Soon, though, he was doing no more than unwrapping them, glancing at the opening lines and replacing them in the sheath.

Christian dropped the last scroll back into the bag, stood, and looked intently at Messenger.

"It's the entire book of Psalms," he declared, as he watched Messenger for some hint of explanation.

"No. Not all. Perhaps one-third."

"Why have you shown them to me?"

"No great reason," came the reply, as Messenger lifted the sack and turned away. "Although," he added almost as an afterthought, "I thought you might be interested in seeing the music room in which they were penned."

Chapter 6

"The time is that of Solomon. The place is near the City of God, but our destination is that stone quarry," said Messenger.

Chris and Messenger made their way down the crest of a steeply slanting hill. As they descended, Chris caught sight of a plateau that seemed to contain an innumerable quantity of huge stones. Beyond the plateau was a vast hole where, obviously, the stones had been cut.

As they approached the scattered stones, Christian tried to peer over the top, a task he found just barely possible.

Each stone was in a different stage of completion. Some were still shapeless masses of rock, others were huge rectangles, rough and jagged. Still others were glass smooth on one or two sides, while still coarse on the others. A few were complete, six sides almost glistening in smooth perfection.

On and on they walked, past hundreds, perhaps thousands, of stones. Christian began to wonder where the workers were and was about to ask when suddenly they came to the edge of a gigantic hole. It was the former mountain, now a vast pit, where the stones were first cut from rock. There in the quarry itself were several hundred workers. A rough stone was just being pulled free of the mother mountain. For a long time they watched as laborers and masons plied their skill to move the rough rock to higher ground.

"After the stone is cut free of the earth it is pulled

here to the flat of the earth. The stone is then cut to an exact, predetermined size, chiseled with large, coarse cutting instruments until it has some semblance of shape, then cut with finer chisels." Messenger paused, looked at Christian, then continued. "Next it is coarse sanded, then it is fine sanded, and last polished."

Christian made no response, but was obviously listening earnestly to be sure he grasped any hidden meaning.

"When the stone mason is finished, the stone is flawless. From here the stone is then taken to a distant city and to a building site. All these stones will be taken to that city. Each is destined to be taken to an already predetermined place. It is interesting, Christian, that when this happens each stone fits perfectly into its place." Messenger paused. "They fit so perfectly in fact, that they appear to be but *one* stone."

"One stone. *One* stone?" mumbled Christian looking about at an endless array of thousands of rocks and stones. "One," he repeated.

"What kind of building is it, some sort of shrine?" queried Christian.

"No," said Messenger as he peered over one of the completed stones. "No, a house. You might call it a home. I would refer to it as a home. A place for someone to live. That is, someone *and* his family."

"A king?"

"Yes, you might call him that, I suppose."

"But there are enough stones here to build a city! A very, very large city," Christian protested.

"Very observant," replied Messenger. "Oh, one other thing," continued Messenger, as he moved across to the stone nearest Christian. He reached down and picked up a hammer and chisel. "Can you hear the masons? They are beginning to return to their work over there. Hear the hammers? The chisels?

"One day, when all these stones are completed, they will be taken to the site, near the house. There they will be taken through a door, and from there to the building site itself . . . where the stones are being re-assembled." Messenger dropped his voice and continued slowly, as if to make his point very clear. "Re-assembled, but this time into a house . . . almost as one vast stone.

"Anyway, at that site, young Christian, on *that* side of the door, there will be no hammer, no chisel, no mason work at all. It is here, on this side of the building site where all cutting, chiseling, sanding and polishing *must* take place.

"Here! *Not* there. All the thud of hammer and falling of axes, the grating of chisels and the grinding of sand . . . is done *here*!

"It is the plan of the Masterbuilder that all the business of making rough rock into perfectly fitting, polished stone be accomplished in the stone quarry. *There*, there, beyond this place, beyond that door, is only the assembling together of what has been done *here*."

"Messenger, I'm stuck. I understand what you've just said, I really do. But I'm stuck on the size of that king's house. There is enough stone here to build a house the size of a metropolis."

"You are right," Messenger replied as he lifted both hands. "This particular house is large. Large enough to be a city, for it shall be a house for God to live in. And in mysteries beyond your finite understanding, that house is a woman, that woman is a bride, and the bride will become a wife. The wife of the King.

"Now, I shall show you yet another quarry." With that Messenger let drop his arms as one might drop a stage curtain. Suddenly everything was pitch black.

Chapter 7

"Great gravy!" exclaimed Christian. "We're in outer space!"

"Correct, young Christian. Now, please turn around. Carefully, look behind and below you. But do not be afraid. You will not fall."

"I don't believe it. That's earth. It's like I'm standing on a space platform . . . that isn't there."

Messenger paid no heed to Christian's exclamations.

"It is a mystery, this thing," mused Messenger, speaking almost as if to himself.

"What," asked Christian, the uncertainty of his footing reflected in the unsteadiness of his voice.

"Here is the real quarry," said Messenger, pointing to earth. You are down there somewhere, being chiseled on by God, man and circumstances. But not you alone. Every believer who has ever lived, those who lived before *His* visitation and all those who are yet to come, one day you all will be lifted out of this quarry through that door . . ."

Christian whirled around in the direction Messenger was pointing, but saw nothing.

"*Then* shall no hammer be heard, for all of that is done in the quarry. Nor shall you be there as an endless array of stones. But together you will be assembled in one place, as one. A living city . . . the bride. The New Jerusalem."

"We who live there," again Messenger pointed

toward the door that wasn't, "we await that day with great expectation.

"Christian, there is but one place you will ever learn to follow Him, to worship Him, to obey Him, to love Him. Only one place, one time . . . to love Him. Only one opportunity to be changed into His image. The place is *there*. The time . . . your 70 years."

Christian said nothing, but only stared at the planet far below him. Finally, he whispered, "A quarry. I live in the midst of a quarry. Called earth."

Messenger placed his hand firmly on Christian's shoulder. "Rose petals falling on a rock never made it a precious stone," he said softly. "Constant joy never produced a transformed . . ."

"I understand," replied Christian.

"Good," said Messenger. There was a long pause. When Messenger spoke again it was with a foreboding that sent a chill through Christian.

"Now we must return to earth. We will be in a place I prefer neither to visit nor even consider. Come. But be warned, Christian, in that place I make poor company."

Chapter 8

Christian found himself standing on the tile roof of a house in some ancient city. Somehow Christian knew he was standing on this spot, facing in this direction, for some particular reason.

"I've never felt anything like this in my life," said Christian. "It's like evil and danger were hanging in the air."

With doom almost dripping from his voice, Messenger responded. "We will not stay here long, Christian. There are disadvantages to be found in the mastery of time and space.

"You stand at a point where sin, wickedness, death, and even hell have intersected. Christian, you are in Jerusalem . . . on the blackest day of her history."

"Jerusalem," murmured Christian in awe.

"But it is not the city that has brought us here. There, toward the north, beyond the wall."

"I can't see anything. It's too far away. Besides, it's getting inky dark over there."

"It is better not to be too near that cursed place. Further, it is not for you to see, but only to hear."

At that instant, a piercing, woeful cry went up that reached into the bowels of Christian, shaking every corpuscle of his being. Messenger crossed his arms over his face and fell to his knees. Christian found himself clutching at his face with both hands. Each was engulfed in a sense of agonizing, unbearable sorrow.

Blackness fell over the hill. The earth began to roll in waves. The roof on which they stood began to crumble.

"Messenger, please, get us out of this place. I don't belong here. I can feel it, I don't belong here. Please."

Messenger stood, immobile, staring relentlessly into Christian's terrorized eyes. Christian sensed displeasure in Messenger's whole being.

"Mortal," spoke Messenger in a voice that would have menaced an archangel. "You find it so easy to be dissatisfied with God because you do not understand His ways in you. You, who have even entertained the thought of displeasure at a God who doesn't explain His ways. Listen now, mortal, and understand . . . even the Son of God is not spared from the abandonment of God. Shall you then be?"

Messenger continued. "A moment ago your Savior died. He died the incarnation of sin, swallowed up in the iniquity of all mankind. In the final madness of that flood, even He was unsure."

"Unsure of what?"

"Of what? Of all things."

Messenger paused, his eyes burning in his head. "Of what, Christian? Of this: He was unsure He would rise from the dead. Without uncertainty, without unanswered questions, there is no such thing as the cross."

Chapter 9

The darkness grew. Soon Chris could see nothing but the dark before his eyes. The sounds faded with the light. For a moment Chris thought he was back to that place before time, where his journey had first begun. Then he heard Messenger speak, his voice coming from some distance away.

"We stand just outside the threshold of that time when the new creation had its smallest and earliest beginning. I will leave you now. But I will return. We shall have one more journey together."

Immediately Chris sensed that the strange darkness surrounding him had given way to earth's ordinary night. Chris was standing at a window looking out into a starry night.

Chris turned to get his bearings. He was back in his room. Messenger was gone. Lying on the bed was a letter and a package. Someone had brought them to his room during this strange interlude. Chris picked up the letter. The postmark was Wales, the sender was Marta Young. He tore open the envelope.

Dear Chris:

I talked to your Dad and Mother by phone about two weeks ago. I'm sure they have given you the details of Bill's death. Frankly none of us expected this, despite the pending operation.

I am handling it pretty well. We had 27 wonderful years together. I still have the memory of Bill, and I am still part of this dear fellowship here in Bangor where Bill labored so long. Also, I still have Christ.

Chris, under separate cover I am sending some things for you that were from Bill. I think, though, I'd better explain. During Bill's last months he was in bed almost constantly. He kept a yellow note pad next to his bed. Every once in a while he would have a thought, reach for the pad, and scribble a note to you.

I don't know whether to say he has written about seven letters to you or about 50! I've not tried to change anything, the letters are sent to you exactly as he wrote them.

He was also working on a short article during this time. I've made a copy and am sending it to you along with his letters.

I hope, between the letters and manuscript, you will find some help in your new Christian life.

I plan to return to the States next summer for a visit. When I drop in to see Bud perhaps you'll be home from school and we can talk.

Your aunt, by law—

> Your sister, by grace,
> Marta

Part II

Chapter 10

Dear Chris:

I've been lying here in bed trying to think of a way to begin this correspondence. Perhaps the best way for us to understand the Lord's way of transformation in our lives is to understand what we are like internally.

We are almost, but not quite, two people: an outer man and an inner man. Your inner man tends toward the spiritual, your outer man tends toward the physical. Each has its own strengths and its own weaknesses. Your Lord wishes to strengthen the inward man and, in some ways, to weaken or at least bring into submission the outer man. When you are a young Christian you will do everything you can to help Him; yet there is little if anything you can do except get in the way. The problem after age 28-32 is the very opposite. You will find, in your early thirties, a temptation to prevent your Lord from doing His work in strengthening the spirit and subduing the strength of the outer man. Take heart; that age between 30-35 gets a bit more realistic about the cross, about suffering, and about the Lord. But whether you be in your twenties agreeing, or your thirties resisting, or vice versa, young or old, the truth is—virtually everything done toward transformation... He will do!

How will He change you? He will work in you two ways: by a cross from without, working inwardly through body and soul; and by His Spirit at the very inmost center of your being, working outwardly through your spirit and soul. (I trust you see that *His* cross and *His* spirit converge on *your* soul.)

When I was a little boy, I tried to imagine what the very center of the earth was like. I envisioned a place in the very heart of the earth about the size of a ball that was the true center. I realized that ball would show virtually no movement. There is a central place in you just like that. From that inmost place God will work His way outward. A work that has not passed through your spirit into your soul is not a work that is God.

There will be times when the Lord will seek to do His desire in you. He will start with the inward man, but as the Spirit works His way outward, He will encounter a soul that is already quite occupied with something else. It is here that not only the spirit will work in the soul, but the cross will also come to hew out a place in the soul large enough for the spirit to find new room.

This takes time, a long time. I remind you that very little of the Lord's transformation work is accomplished in your twenties. The inward man and the outward man have a hard time getting along with each other. There is independent action on the part of both. One must enlarge. By the nature of things, one life must recede. If it is the more earthly part of you and not the "other dimensional" part of you that grows stronger and stronger, the realm of the spirituals (at the center of your being) will tend to diminish. At best, the spiritual element in you will be able to do no more than rattle your conscience from time to time. How shall you encourage the growth of the spiritual implant within you? Well, how much are you willing to cooperate with the divine moving of another life form?

The Lord would cause a reversal in the roles of those two forms of life. He would have that spiritual realm in you controlling the more visible realm. He is after that which dwells within the inmost part of you holding sway over that which dwells primarily in your outward parts.

* * * * *

Where does the human portion of you live, Chris? The human part of you lives within your soul. The Scripture seems to indicate that there is even some element within the soul that must be put to death; therefore, at a minimum, the Christian faith recognizes that the soul—or some portion in the soul—needs to be dealt with. But how? If you seek to suppress the dark side of your soul, it will be suppressed, but only in that one place. You may be sure that dark thing will come out in another part of your personality. There is a difference between that person who suppresses things and one who has been truly dealt with by the Lord.

For 33 years, the Lord's relationship with the Father included the relationship of His soul with the Father's own Spirit. To put it another way, the Lord's human life had a relationship to the Father's divine life. (I suppose I need not state the obvious, that the Lord Jesus also had a relationship in His Spirit with the Father; His Divine Life was one with the life of the Father.) What of that relationship? Was the Lord suppressing His soul? No, not at all. For Him it was a matter of His soul being in submission to Divine Life.

This, essentially, is His goal in you. The human element of you, in submission to the divine portion that was planted in you at conversion.

Chapter 11

Chris:

When God looks inside you with eyes that see spiritual things, He looks upon a whole different world than does a doctor who sees only material things.

Imagine your inner workings something like this. The spirit has been implanted deep within you. Around your spirit is something that is probably a little bit hard, your human nature or soul. The spirit wishes to gain control of the human element, but that thing called the soul seems, by the nature of the Fall, to contain something in it that is not at all in agreement with this project. The religious part of the soul will acquiesce immediately, or so it seems. Truthfully, from the moment of acquiescence on, the religious part of you will do everything it possibly can to prevent a takeover by the spirit. That self portion of the soul will do everything it can to resist the growth of the spirit within your inward parts. The self nature knows it is marked for death. (Self is generally referred to as that part of the soul that got there by sin being introduced into man by the Fall.) If the spirit penetrates outwardly, the self element of the soul is in trouble. The mind may (or may not) agree with this project, but it will come up with a thousand reasons, all of which it will blame on God and the Scripture, for not getting too involved. The emotions will ascend and rejoice in this project and then scream to high heaven and cry at its very first loss.

Later the emotions may even turn belligerent against a meany of a God who would treat it so indelicately. Our emotions sometimes author one of the greatest problems of our Christian life: to create a God in its own image, a loving, sweet, and precious God who wouldn't dare declare war on a person's dominant emotions. The emotions do not have a franchise on this project. The intellect often sculpts out a God in its own image, a God who is very intelligent, rational, reasonable, very logical, very scriptural, very boxable and definable, and having erected this mind-made God in the center of life, will vow and declare that this, and this alone, is the true and living God.

What of the strong-willed person? He will tie his ambitions, whatever they are, in with being transformed. With that rather dubious consecration, the Christian has several avenues he can take: becoming very, very réligious, praying constantly, embracing anything that looks like the cross and driving everybody in sight half crazy. Unconsciously, he sincerely believes he will be able to will into being his transformation, no matter how many times you tell him this is a matter that is God's alone. When he at last stumbles and falls in the middle of Romans 7, he may get very, very hostile toward the God who has allowed him to fail so miserably so many times. Or hopefully, that strong will may break under the hand of God who will not allow anyone to succeed in the Christian life by his own exertions.

What is my point? Human life, regardless of the way it manifests itself, really isn't all that obedient to the project of being divinely absorbed.

Isn't that wonderful?

What a great day it is when that inmost strength of

a man's created life breaks. After that he will find it very easy to relate to his Lord, be he primarily emotional, mindy, or willful. Gradually there will come into focus a God not made in his own image: emotional, intellectual or willful. The true Lord cuts across all three of those major characteristics of man.

Somehow, when the spirit begins to gain control of the soul, be it ever so gradual, none of these three characteristics will dominate. Rather, ever after, the things that touch your outer person will not be quite so successful in influencing the inner man. Counterwise, that inmost man will be far more likely to dominate the outer man. As the years go by, if you are doubly blessed by the Lord, perhaps that which is divine in the inmost part will have so completely flooded the outer man that some portions of the outer man are indistinguishable from the inmost man.

That, dear Chris, entails a great deal of *the Lord's* workings in both your soul and spirit.

Chapter 12

Chris:

I reflect back on my seminary education. I took my seminary work in one of the finest theological institutions in the world. Nor would I disparage that place or the fine men who taught me. Nonetheless, except for the fact that we were all poor and suffered the results of that particular problem, I saw and heard very little about the deep internal work of the cross. But perhaps that is as it should be, for you cannot teach the cross. Not really.

If a student of theology were to decide to give his entire life to the study of the cross, never by such means would he lay hold of transformation. Neither theology, nor gift, nor knowledge—even *scriptural* knowledge—is of real benefit in the destruction of those things within us that must be destroyed. At some point, you and the Lord have to get down to practical business. There must be lostness, there must be pain, there must be hurt, there must be tears. And on our part there probably must be even confusion, discouragement, tests, trials, hopelessness and perhaps the sense that the Lord no longer loves us. Perhaps a sense even deeper, darker and more foreboding than that. The cross is primarily an experiential thing. All the discussion in the world concerning it can never describe what being nailed to it is really like.

Christendom is full of a lot of workers, semi-workers, would-be workers and just plain old ordinary Christians who are ambitious: Christians who think that they are qualified to serve the Lord because they have stacks of notebooks full of information. I'm constantly amazed how we equate the matter of knowing information with being qualified to serve the Lord. A seminary education is certainly an excellent demonstration of that. I enrolled in seminary at a very young age. A lady who took my application at the desk thought there had been a mistake, that no one *that* young could be allowed into the seminary. But because I was a college graduate, they let me in. After I had spent a year there on Seminary Hill and learned all sorts of marvelous things (all aimed straight at my frontal lobe), I began to be called Reverend. I even began to be treated in a more pious, holy manner by other people. What holy thing had happened to me? Nothing except I had been exposed to an enormous amount of information which had accumulated over the last 1,000 years. But nothing inside me had changed from the mere fact that I had acquired that information. In the seminary I attended, I was surrounded by 2,000 other young men and young women who were also piling up a lot of information. I recall no one being changed by it, though.

The teaching may be right, but there will be very little to supply your true and deep needs unless your inner workings have been transformed. My primary need was not a seminary education but the transformation of my soul. That happens by my soul having a divine encounter which emits from my spirit.

I'm sure you have heard the illustration of Balaam and his donkey. That donkey was so much wiser than the prophet. The donkey could see realms unseen. He could see an angel standing before him. That poor dumb prophet only knew how to conduct morning and evening offerings and how to lift up oxen, bulls, goats and doves on an altar. He was a great speaker, but his inward man didn't operate. Tragically, he could not see the unseen. He had information, but he was not full of things that had come from another realm. He reminds me of the great majority of Christian workers.

The assimilation of more Bible information, more retreats, more sermons, archaeology, theology and all the rest will not add one iota to your deep inward center. Chris, education makes no contribution *there* whatsoever! The dearest, most uneducated, illiterate little lady in the world who knows how to turn and live in hidden realms has more true grasp of the ways of God than all the information hidden in the largest theological library on this continent.

* * * * *

Which would you rather work with? A really smart person, or a really compassionate person? You probably would be better off with neither. A very smart person, a very intelligent person, is usually governed by his mind. A compassionate person might be under the influence of his emotions. If you were to work with the ideal person, it would be someone who is controlled by his spirit. By his spirit. Now that is wholly another dimension, something otherworldly, something not of this planet. The Scripture tells us our thoughts are not His thoughts, our ways are not His ways. When we speak of living by the spirit, we are speaking of living by a means not human. We are speaking of something that has to do with divinity and with other realms.

But maybe we should turn the question around.

When someone looks at you and they think of working with you, what comes to their mind?

We are told by those who study mankind that, dispositionally, we each fall into three basic catagories: the doers, the feelers, the thinkers. This is the human side of us. The Lord wants us to be controlled, not by our emotions, or thoughts, or will, but by our spirit.

And how are you to be controlled by your spirit? To bring you to where you live in that realm . . . in your spirit . . . *that* is a project God has had underway ever since the moment you received Jesus Christ as your Lord and Savior. There is no way that I can describe to you exactly what it means to be led by your spirit or to be governed by the inmost part of your being. I can tell you it's a little different from being primarily under the control of your thoughts, or primarily under the control of your emotions, or primarily under the control of your strength of will. Nor can I tell you exactly how you arrive at living by your spirit. But I can tell you this: In order for that day to come, a lot of changes will be wrought in your life regardless of whether you are primarily volitional, emotional, or mental.

When three newly converted Christians start on the adventure of the Christian life, one being rather emotional, another rather strong in his determination, and the third seeming to carry everything about life in his head, not one of these has an advantage over the other two. The truth of the matter is, each one will have to be taken out of that which is his primary characteristic. Or, to state it clearly, whatever you are, *that* has to be broken.

God isn't primarily will, nor emotions, nor intellect . . . so He favors none of these. Generally speaking, divinity professors favor one, the charismatic leader favors yet another, and the evangelist who wishes to convert the world yet another. But God isn't a divinity professor, a charismatic leader nor an evangelist . . . nor is He primarily human. He is God.

And how shall He break the will of the evangelist, subdue the emotions of the charismatic, and goodness knows what to the intellect? By making available to each of them an abundance of encounters with other realms—the spiritual, that is, the heavenly places—which are in Christ Jesus. *And* also by a great deal of the cross, plunged like a knife at the very center of the soul.

What is it He is seeking to deal with in you? If you are the intellectual type, that is what he will be going after. If you are the emotional type, He will be seeking to balance that. If you are one strong in volition, He will be out to break the strength of your will. What will He do? Make the emotional person intellectual, and the intellectual person an emotional person? No. He will be seeking to weave something else into you that is characterized not primarily by either a keen mind, deep feelings or a strong will. Rather, He will be seeking to introduce into you the characteristics of a species that comes from outer space. I assure you that that species, nay, that *Person* is not someone who is technologically more advanced nor more (or less) emotional than fallen man. All science fiction stories notwithstanding, *that* species comes not from out there somewhere in the sky but from another realm, and He is just a little bit different from the thinker, the feeler or the doer.

In the transformation of that part of us which is so very human by that which is so divine, I do not mean to leave the impression that you will one day become some sort of a human vegetable. Not at all. The emotions are still there, the intellect is still there and the will is still there. Feelers, doers and thinkers are changed, not eliminated. These elements in their lives will become servants of another life, the divine life in the inmost man.

So, I recommend that (1) you have a lot of encounters with Christ, and (2) you prepare for an onslaught of the cross.

Chapter 13

Chris:

In every generation there have been men who have emphasized how much blessing there is in Christ. In our day this has come to be called "the prosperity gospel." On the other hand there are those who always present the suffering of the Christian life to the point of morbidity. These, I suppose, could be called Christian masochists. The problem is that there is truth in both claims but, be sure, the prosperity gospel has always sold better than the cross.

Young Christians are always surprised, and even amazed, at the extent to which the Lord allows suffering in each of our lives. (So are old ones!) Those who have been raised on a prosperity gospel are very susceptible to having their faith destroyed when life, the world, sin, weakness, family problems, poor health and a myriad of other things come crashing down on them.

A young Christian who, at the beginning of his conversion, has the privilege of gathering with a group of Christians who are really close-knit . . . well, after a while he might begin to see all the problems the group has and conclude, "It is impossible that God is here. There is just too much sorrow."

Chris, if you happen to have been exposed to the world of the prosperity gospel, then you need to look up and realize that the God who created you is also the Father of Jesus Christ, and He did not spare Him of

His suffering. Nor the twelve, nor the gentile churches, nor . . . well . . . anyone! If you have been told that Christ took all your problems so that you might be totally free, then I would remind you that the founding fathers of your faith suffered greatly, and seeing you in a distant mist, spoke of your suffering, too. In fact, they even guaranteed your sufferings.

(As has been often noted, the prosperity gospel is invalid and even ridiculous when preached outside of the industrial nations of the West.) I have to admit that those who follow a prosperity gospel seem to prosper and have more fun than the rest of us might. On the other hand, I personally have not yet encountered a deep work of Christ woven into the life of anyone who strongly pursues a prosperity gospel. The Lord has a way of seeing that we get the desires of our heart. If we desire prosperity, we will probably have it. If we desire transformation, He will even more quickly accommodate us! That's because transformation is closer to His own heart than prosperity ever could be.

Most of us do not live the hilarious Christian life all the time. The traffic lights are not always green, the job promotion is not always given, health is not always near perfect. Even in the matter of healing, the vast majority of us walk around with portions of our body very much unhealed. In the midst of our troubles we invariably meet our smiling brother who tells us that the Lord has died for us in such a way that we should never be ill. He boasts that such is his own lot in life. We grit our teeth and wonder whether to believe him or to believe our instinct. (One thing is certain: Chris, don't discuss the Scripture with him on this subject. There are ample verses in the Bible to prove anything, anybody, anywhere at any time wants to believe about anything.)

As a young Christian you will be tempted to join the prosperity club. As a mature one you'll be glad you didn't.

If you are one of those who is truly sold on the idea of a gospel that always prospers, always heals, then perhaps you should read what befell those we generally refer to as the cream of the crop.

Some tortured, refusing deliverance.
(They received a better resurrection.)
Yet others put on trial with cruel mocking
   and whipppings.
Others bound and imprisoned.
Others stoned.
Others sawed into pieces.
Tempted.
Slain with a sword.
Wandering about in sheep's skins and goat skins.
Destitute.
Afflicted.
Tormented.

Where in the world was God when all this was happening? And where was the prosperity gospel?

If you wish to follow the Lord to the uttermost, *and* if you wish also to embrace a gospel of constant blessing, health and prosperity, then perhaps you should reconsider the whole matter of following the Lord.

The most awesome thing about that list of men and women and their sufferings is this: Not one of those believers had what you have—not one of them had the indwelling Christ. That list, as you know, is of Old Testament followers! Truly, their faithfulness is astounding.

Why their suffering? The reasons are many. Perhaps one of the main reasons they suffered was to be a witness to you, the new covenant pilgrim.

* * * * *

I challenge the idea that suffering is first of all a punishment for our sins. If that were true, then every believer on earth would be hiding under a rock somewhere. Which of us really deserves less punishment than the next? If you really think there are some Christians who are generally a lot more righteous and devoted, loving and kind, gracious and gentle than others, then you have underestimated the Fall.

No, it is not a punishment, Chris. He is doing something in you for eternity. He is doing something in you for your own life, *now*: *and* He is doing something in you that in not only for *your* life *now*, but also for the church, which is His bride, that she might be made entire and complete, now!

The Lord knows something we don't: The Fall has left *all* of us in dire straits. Most of us are either extremely sinful or extremely religious. Or both! And further, I suspect that neither one of those states pleases God more than the other. Neither impresses Him. What *He* does in us impresses Him!

He knows something else: We usually learn about *Him* only during periods of adversity. Few, if any, of us really seek after a deep, intimate relationship with the Lord except (1) just before, (2) during, and (3) right after those periods of calamity, disaster, catastrophe, suffering and pain! That's true of the very sinful, the very religious, and . . . well . . . the rest of us!

Impressive lot, we Christians!

Thank God He knows us. Thank God He works with us the way He does.

The Jews always thought that affliction had something to do with sin in one's life. The whole book of Job points out the fallacy of that idea. But that kind of an idea dies hard. Until this very day you can be sure that there will be someone to come by and tell you that the woe-begotten thing that has happened to you is the direct result of sin (or disobedience) in your life. Shades of Job's friends! Doesn't anybody ever read that book?

My own observation has been that the wicked, the sinful, the backslidden either fare no worse than the best of Christians or, in a remarkable number of cases, fare even better! True, the Lord may get your attention with chastisement, but He is not a God who goes around striking people with horrible plagues if they have not obeyed Him perfectly. You would be wise, Chris, to look for some other reason for your problems before you embrace the punishment theory. (I confess to you that in my 30-year career as a Christian sinner I don't recall the Lord ever severely punishing me for a sin I committed.)

Be sure, affliction that comes into your life carries with it a word from the Lord. Beyond that, suffering from the Lord has a disciplinary effect upon the life of *any* believer. The Lord is seeking to transform every portion of the bride of Christ so that her totality might be something that matches the very Son of God.

And where might you expect this disciplinary work of God to fall into your life? The Lord will sometimes touch your *spirit*, sometimes it will be your *soul*, and sometimes it will be your *body*.

When we see the martyrdom, the persecution, the

blood, the crying, the wails, the tears, the depth, the length, the breadth of the agony of the body of Christ through the years, it boggles the mind. And yet, some-one else looked upon this scene and saw something else entirely. He saw as one does when he is viewing things from other realms. From *that* view he declared in Holy Writ:

> These light afflictions
> Are working for you
> An eternal weight of glory.

* * * * *

Whatever it is He sends and whenever it falls, it is a light affliction and it works an exceedingly great work. It produces internal, eternal glory. Whatever it is the Lord puts into your life, that affliction is a friend work-ing *for* you, not against you.

Chapter 14

Dear Chris:

We walk a thin line when we talk about either the *joy* of the Christian life or the *cross* of the Christian life. Either can be over-emphasized. You can be sure that your own natural inclinations will find expression here. The more positive person will gravitate toward the positive thoughts, things of joy and exuberance. The more inward person will find happiness in the gloom of his considerations of the cross. Neither view is truly Christian; both these outlooks are dispositional.

The soul under the Lord's control, whether that soul be exuberant by nature or gloomy by nature, will be, to some degree, altered in its attitude. The cross doesn't go around altering the joy bug to gloom. The cross alters the gloom bug, too. Both are changed—transformed—*toward* the mark! Let's say you are a young Christian with a morose nature. Somewhere along the way—in God's scheme of things—you must learn that even the cross of Christ must sometimes go to the cross. You will need to place your cross syndrome on the cross. Let's say you are of a more exuberant nature. You may find—somewhere along the way—that the Lord will work a balance. How? I do not know. I would venture this much, probably by the bludgeoning work of a pitiless cross.

So, both the optimist and the pessimist are in for a divine adjustment. He displaces *all* human disposition with a divine one.

There is a strong human element in each of us. In the silent, the loud, the neurotic, the well balanced. Yes, all of us. Some portion of the earthen part of each Christian needs its energies and abilities and understandings transformed to something higher. Before that higher point arrives, the soul may go through some rough days.

Do not fall into the trap of trying to suppress your soul—or personally hauling it to the cross, there to scrounge around for a hammer and some nails. The Lord Himself needs no help. You will only get in His way. Besides, I don't think I would be too wide of the mark to say to you that His higher purpose in you is not so much to make your soul weak as it is to make your spirit strong.

* * * * *

Somewhere deep down within you, everything that Christ has ever gone through is already deposited in you. *Some* of that which is His experience He desires that *you* also experience. He has a yoke to place around your neck. It is an easy yoke; that is a guarantee, for He has already gained the strength to bear that yoke.

Some of His experience has to do with sufferings, but you will never know suffering to the extent He did. You fill up only *part* of His suffering; yet, you are the recipient of all the strength He won in His sufferings. (Granted, Chris, the strength *never* seems to arrive at the most needy moment.) You have within your inmost being, right now, the divine life of God. You also have within your being—a little closer to the surface—the human life given to you by your mother and father. The life they gave you was fallen. These two lives, one human life and the other divine life, cannot possibly live inside you in total harmony. The two are vastly different life forms.

Sometimes they go in opposite directions, operating totally different from one another, just as bird life differs from lion life. There are times when your human life easily relates to that divine life. At still other times your soul is neutral to that life. Unfortunate, but true, at other times—wittingly or unwittingly—your human life moves in the opposite direction of that higher life. At *that* point your soul will most likely encounter the cross.

Chapter 15

Dear Chris:

What kind of person can best endure suffering?

Quite frankly, once suffering takes up residence, it seems none of us are qualified. Why? Suffering that comes from the hand of God seems to be so selected, so tailored for the one to whom it is sent. The thing you might shoulder the easiest may never come to you; but that one weakness you were never prepared for, that one hidden portion of your life you probably didn't even know about—*there* is where the blow will fall.

Years ago a grand old gentleman of the faith came to visit me when I was very ill. At that time I had been in bed for nearly a year. As we talked, I shared with him my feelings, my doubts, and the whole agony of it all. It was a cataract of complaint, doubt and question. I could speak freely to him because I knew that he had once been in bed for a long time with an extreme case of TB. In the great wisdom of my 32 years, I said something like this to him: "I'm too young for this to happen to me. It should have come sometime in the future. You were 40 when it happened to you. You knew the Lord a lot better than I do. I was just beginning to learn a little bit about Him and His ways and then *this* happened. I'm not equipped, I'm not the type, and I'm not ready. I'm too young, too inexperienced, not Christian enough to handle this thing."

He looked at me in astonishment and replied, "I was 40, and that was too young, too."

What kind of Christian can best endure suffering? He doesn't exist. I could handle your problems easily. You could handle mine with a yawn. But it didn't happen that way. I got the ones *I* couldn't handle; so did you.

Chapter 16

Dear Chris:

This morning two Christian roommates got up at 5:00 a.m. and prayed together for an hour. Now it is around 11:00 a.m. and roommate Number 1 is telling roommate Number 2 that he shouldn't play "that kind of music"; or is it a book that is sinful? Or is roommate #2 being told he should not go to a picnic this afternoon? Whatever, roommate #1 is a legalist. On the other hand, roommate #2 is getting very indignant. "That's none of your business. I'm free in Christ to do any and all things," may be what roommate #1 is about to hear. Here's another possibility: Roommate #2 remains very quiet, bearing the burden of outrage and unjust persecution with grace!

There is only one thing certain about this scene. There is absolutely nothing going on in it that is divine activity. (Unless it is God's humor in casting together these two young Christian opposites as roommates.)

What can be done to prevent scenes like that? They occur every day among singles. Nothing really. Trying to take the religious nature out of a single brother in his twenties would be very much like trying to take the bones out of his body. It's part of the package!

Let us hope that the passing of time will teach them compassion. I fervently hope some older man my age doesn't encourage their religiosity. Just as fervently, I hope some older brother does not step in and try to pass rules against such blatant immature religiosity.

What can be done? Not much. One year of marriage will end a lot of single brotherness. Time and the cross are the two greatest needs of these two young men. The cross seems to be the great equalizer and leveler of all single brothers!

In a few years one of two things will happen to these two young men. They will be harsh, critical and controlling men—or they will have become so embittered by what they went through as young people they will have left both that fellowship and the kingdom and the Lord. Or, they will sit around one night and laugh uproariously at how unbelievably religious they were when they were young and thank their Lord for every maturing experience they went through.

Lord, hasten the day when the world is filled with such men. Men whose bowels are filled with grace, compassion, love, liberty and freedom and have the wisdom—as older men— to guide tenderly and forbear in the lives of some very religious young men and women who got up to pray together this morning, optimistic, enthusiastic and full of blind faith. May God keep them ever so.

Still, the fact remains, they *are* sons of a fallen race. In them, and in you, Chris, there is something very self-centered that will never die except for the jabbing pains of adversity. If you resist, if you hold on to that deep self-centered place, ever guarding it, making sure that it is not invaded even by the hand of God, then something in you will go unchanged and unbroken throughout all of your life upon this earth. An altar, a throne room, an inner sanctuary where self is worshipped will never be cast down. Be sure, my young brother, one day the Lord will lift the hand of protection from you and out of love He will say, ''Now I will allow this one to suffer.'' On that day you will begin to fellowship with Christ in His sufferings. Those sufferings had purpose in His earthly life, they will just as certainly have purpose in yours.

You should recognize that the entrance of pain into your life is antagonistic to the dark side of your human nature. The two are natural enemies. But there will be very little, if any, spiritual progress in the deeper parts of you until the deadly, cold blade of the cross pierces to the vitals of a self-nature buried so deeply and woven so completely into your human nature they seem to be one and the same.

Chapter 17

Dear Chris:

Perhaps the best way to illustrate one of the things the Lord must do in all of our lives is to use the example of what He does to the extremely gifted. If the Lord will bring the cross to a well balanced Christian who loves Him, surely He will visit us all. There comes immediately to my mind Christian workers.

Here is a man—or woman—who is extraordinarily gifted. He speaks so well, he writes well, he is socially very attracting, he has a deep insight into the Scripture. He has everything together. I often stand back, observe and shudder as I consider what God must do to such a man to break him. Well I might. An ancient gray-headed lady of the cross once stepped back . . . and shuddered . . . as I fervently requested that God break me, and she contemplated the horror story which she was sure would come to my life if ever He set out to answer my prayer.

We know it is terribly important that the Christian worker be broken. If for no other reason, we need to be reassured that one who can speak so eloquently of Christ really loves Him. Does he love the Lord enough to still love Him when all his gifts, which helped him make Christ so attractive, are taken away from him? Will he love the Lord when he has nothing? And *then*, love Him still? If he does not love the Lord that much, then we really don't want to hear from him or follow him.

Brokenness is more dearly prized by the Lord than all of the greatness this world has ever seen. The only way anyone breaks is by having a great deal of pressure applied to him . . . usually at his strongest point. Success never meant a great deal in the kingdom of God, certainly not from His viewpoint, at least. The greater things which have come to your Lord have come as a result of overwhelming disaster. The fall. The cross. These led to redemption. A new creation. A bride.

There will be no meekness and compassion without disaster and loss. There will be no unselfishness without a mortal blow dealt to selfishness. There will be no humility until there is a total and irreparable loss of reputation. There will never be any true success in the Lord's work until it has been preceded by many, many turns of disastrous failure.

And you can be sure that the Lord loves you too much to shield you from the uncomfortable.

> It is through a broken heart that God brings
> His purpose into the world.
> Then Lord, bring forth my broken heart.
> Bring forth out of Your treasures
>   my broken heart.

* * * * *

Temporary success in a city has caused many a Christian worker to begin right there to build an empire. Instead he should have built the church of Jesus Christ. Many a Christian worker has raised up a work that perhaps was worthy to be called "church life" or "body life." Once built, problems developed. He fought tooth, tong and nail to preserve his work. Why? I wonder. Why fight to perserve it? It will stand if it is Christ. If part of it stands, and that part is really Christ, then having nothing but that little part surviving is far better than a large work that has to be held together by reason, logic, theology, fear, accusation, doctrine or whatever. In my judgement, the worker might seriously consider stepping back, even out— dying to his work, letting the fire fall on that work and seeing just how much of it can survive.

There are many great success stories around, but those works very rarely reflect the bride of Jesus Christ.

Sometimes, Chris, she seems to be as elusive as her Lord. Rarely do you see her beautiful and whole, gathering somewhere in a city. Rarely will *you* ever gather in a place where you will sense that deep work of Christ in a corporate body of people. Being with a people who have been made one . . . and whose oneness—tested by the long trek of time—is found in nothing, absolutely nothing, but Christ. Such a people is rare, exotically rare. Rare because that glorious work which the Father did in the Son was so rare.

* * * * *

There is no facade that you can build around your life but what the Lord will one day have to come crashing through, be that facade the pearly-white-teeth, trium-phant Christian, or the holy Saint Joe routine. Your Lord will open doors and rip down walls and let in light. Light will fall in places you dare not let any eye behold. Your whole concept of what human life is, your whole concept of what divine life is, and how each of these two lives operate—their standards, their values, their actions and reactions in a given set of circumstances— all such things must be changed. Thank God they *will* be changed, and they will be changed by Him, not you. Changed by a deep work of your indwelling Lord working in your inmost being. He is destined to tear away at the dark side of your soul, at the very strings of your heart, and at the hidden things you hold so dear. It is by the crushing of the idols within your inmost temple that He will make room for the geysers of Divine Life.

* * * * *

The man Job is an enigmatic person. How many wise men have come to his book to seek to find its central theme. And for every man who has picked up a pen to write about Job and his book, a different view has emerged. There is really very little one can say about Job that someone will not disagree with. Unless it be this statement: When the suffering was over, Job was changed.

That is all. It was that simple. When Job's trials were over, Job was changed. That is one sure fact. How God changed him, why God changed him, what was changed is conjecture. But Job *was* a changed man.

Thank you, Friend Pain.

* * * * *

It probably needs to be said here that it really won't be suffering and sorrow and pain that will do the greater part of the work to be done in your life. Actually, these servants of the Lord are only there to bring you to zero. They aid in bringing down that part of you which has been lifted up and in bringing up that which is too far down. It will be in some broken, desperate moment when pain has worked his will in you that you will look up through tearstained, hollow, hopeless eyes and grasp your first true glimpse of the authentic Jesus Christ. It will be in *that* moment, when you have been devastated by an unrelenting God, that you will first come to understand divinity. It will probably be in that moment you will catch a glimpse of Him, untainted by your own dispositional interpretation of what God is like.

And when you stand up, look around you and see that everything has been destroyed; perhaps, for the first time in your life, you will have succeeded! You will have finally caught a pure, unblemished glimpse of Him. Of the One of peerless worth. It is *that* sight which *really* changes us.

The wreckage caused by sorrow and grief
Is the price God is willing to pay
To achieve brokenness, compassion,
And tenderness of spirit in a life that,
In its intrinsic state,
Is a life of unlovingness.

Chapter 18

Dear Chris:

Let's see. I've been serving the Lord now for 30 years. Most of that time has been spent with young people. It is difficult for a worker to communicate to a young believer just how very touchy he really is about his emotions, self-esteem, abilities, quickness, slowness, etc. Generalizing, I would say that as a group you are *very* sensitive. You get your feelings hurt ever so easily, and it is the nature of the beast that once those feelings are hurt, something in the brain starts into a very predictable pattern. You shut down all sane logic, your ears close, your eyes develop tunnel vision, and the only thing you can see, know, feel, hear or think is that someone has treated you unfairly. Internal smoldering begins. Hurt sets in. A new kind of logic comes on the scene, a very blind logic born of a monologue. The offended logic spirals in its rationalization. Your mind so convinces you that you are right you become virtually incapable of grasping the idea that there could be a view different from yours. Behold, you have become an impenetrable fortress of resentment and hurt.

In other words, you are too sensitive! If you are in a close-knit Christian fellowship that is anything remotely similar to church life where Christians are rubbing elbows a lot, I predict that you are going to be devastated. There is a good chance a lot of other people are going to be devastated by whatever process you use to get yourself devastated.

Well, you know the Lord has watched Christians do this for 2,000 years and mankind for a lot longer. Rest assured He has a way to change our natural bent toward getting our feelings hurt. Yes, He can, and does, deal with the super-sensitive nature.

Of course, I haven't seen you in a long time so perhaps you are the opposite type. Are you one of those rare people who never has problems in relating to other people? The problem the rest of us have with you is that you are so subtly self-righteous about the quirks, qualms, peculiarities and downright nuttiness of the rest of us that you drive us crazy.

What is my point? Every son (and daughter) of Adam cherishes his disposition almost more than he treasures anything else on earth, including the Lord. What is worse is the fact that it is a rare man who is even aware of this being a problem.

Here, then, we see a perfect setting for a head-on collision between human life and divine life. Obviously, none of the things I just mentioned are attributes of divine life. The moment human life is put in a bind, it frets! Complains! Gripes! God's life, on the other hand, can lie down upon a cross to be crucified *unjustly* by the very ones whom He created.

But I must balance my words.

There is another kind of Christian who came into focus just as I said, "can lie down upon the cross and be unjustly crucified." There is the Christian who, by his very disposition, tends toward the masochistic. Or who is so super-religious he never complains. Why? Because he is so Christ-like? No, he just enjoys keeping his mouth shut. He likes limited disclosure. It's safe. Literally, it is less painful for him to shut up and be unjustly crucified than to open up and share who he is and what he is going through. (Pity the poor woman who marries him or the roommate who lives with him. He takes to the cross like a duck to water. His wife, in turn, ends up favoring mental institutions.) Somewhere deep down in his unconscious he is very satisfied by the fact that he doesn't blow his cranium every time someone hurts his feelings. Such conduct is neither the denial of the soul nor the Lord working on the outer man. The worst, most horrible, hideous cross that can befall that dear brother (or sister) is for him to have to confront someone else openly or to state openly what is really on his mind. This he will *not* do. He is content. He, like the rest of us, is very proud of his dispositional traits.

Neither the Christian who tends to blow up nor the Chrisitan who tends to stuff it all has met the real cross of Christ.

Ah, take heart, whatever you *really* are, Chris; know that we serve a Lord who loves us enough to go after every trait the soul can display.

When you see how needful all of us are of being changed, how blind and incapable we all are of doing the changing for ourselves, then you are only a short walk over to the place where you can see that every trouble and trial that comes into your life was sent there by the hand of God to accomplish the highest possible good in your life. But you will need all the wisdom of your spirit, all the experience which life has given you to date, plus an awful lot of waiting before God (and perhaps counsel with a Christian friend . . . one who isn't apt to agree with you) to understand how to relate to that hand of God. Somewhere in it all, *know this*: trials are among the greatest blessings of life.

* * * * *

Let me illustrate a bit more what I just said.

I recall the boy who proposed to every girl in his fellowship. I recall the girl who never ceased being boy crazy. What could be done to help them? At the time they were doing these outlandish things, they were also totally given to the Lord. And do you think rebuking them for being so shallow would have helped them? No! Their actions were only symptoms of far deeper, far more inward personality flaws. In both cases, by the way, this flaw was off limits to discussion, sacrosanct. Touch one of those truly basic personality flaws in a believer's life and you will encounter a surprising amount of resistance from some otherwise very dedicated Christian. Fortunately there is one person who refuses to accept these areas as off limits. And when He arrives—always bringing with Him "the worst possible disaster"—the thing He brings into your life is sovereign. You will probably scream bloody-murder, but remember, the problem only looks so bad because it fits your most basic and best protected flaws *so* perfectly.

Chris, expect the Lord to confront you at the point of your greatest weakness.

I think back over what I have seen during these last 15 years when Christians came face to face with a Lord determined to deal with a major flaw. For some, on the very day that they were so confronted, they packed their bags and left . . . the Lord. For others it was a great big sign that said, "Thanks, but no thanks, this is my business not yours." For others it was as un-eventful as being thrown to the lions and ripped apart. The whole fiber of the human being seemed to rend and tear under even the thought of having this dealing introduced into their lives. For others, not only was the psychological nature taxed to its utmost, but even solid marriages twisted, cracked and almost sundered under the weight of just discussing the problem.

Those, dear Chris, are the days when you are *truly* under the sovereign hand of God. There is no thought of looking under rocks to try to find God working in your life. You may well be looking under a rock, all right, for a place to hide. There will be no imitating piety on that day; there will be little ability to look up and say, "Oh, *this* is the Lord." I would sum up the most outstanding characteristic of the dark side of our human nature: It has an almost limitless capacity to survive. I would also sum up your Lord's attitude when He comes for some of the truly major flaws of the soul: He is the only power in the universe more determined to transform you than your soul is to survive. The clash of those two wills is often quite a spectacular event to behold.

* * * * *

Somehow, in God's business of transformation, all these things have to be made level. There has to come a place where virtually nothing done to you, regardless of how unjust it is, can hurt your feelings. By the way, here is another way to know that the Lord has gained some ground in your life: when you can accept criticism, even if viciously served, without a sense of resentment and with no need to retaliate. Turn it around, the hour must come when you are *very* sensitive to *others'* feelings. But I would not recommend you resolve today to always be gentle, sweet and considerate. Better you resolve that your skin turn polka dot—you have a better shot at achieving *that*. No. These are things only pain, heartache and loss can work in your life. And that, only gradually.

Chapter 19

Dear Chris:

And what part does Satan play in all of this?

There is one thing that can be said of Satan. He is about the easiest person in the world to become preoccupied with. There are Christians who are much more enamored with Satan than they are with their Lord. Chris, don't fall into that trap.

We know that one day Satan entered into the chronicle of the life of Jesus Christ. The question of why he appeared has filled volumes, perhaps libraries. This we know: When that confrontation was over, the result which emerged was no less than salvation for all mankind.

Any time you get the idea that God has allowed His enemy some portion of your life, even for one split second, remember this: If God *has* actually allowed Satan to come into your life, when the confrontation is over, the results will be transformation in you. Be sure, a little less of the dark side of your humanity will be there. A little more of the bright side of His divinity will have taken its place.

If you have the tendency to blame everything on the devil, then you're going to miss out on a great deal of the Lord's work intended for your life. In fact, if you have a tendency to blame even a fair size portion of the things that come into your life as something from the devil, you may have missed one of the central issues of God's work in our lives.

True, it may be that this one called Satan is in control of the world; but please remember to press that matter one more step: The Lord is ultimately in control of Satan. I repeat, ultimately, even your enemy Lucifer is under the control of the Lord.

Christian workers especially have a tendency to call anything that opposes their little world and their little work as being from the devil. My, how much of that attitude I have witnessed in these last 30 years.

Such an accusation on the part of a worker, "I'll tell you, this whole thing is of the devil," surely makes it rough on the poor brother who is *really* causing the problem! He wakes up to find all his friends now thinking he's the devil . . . or a reasonable facsimile. It's an uncomfortable feeling, is it not, to be sitting out there in the meeting and hear that what you are doing is "the devil's work." I hope you survive; but frankly the chances are very slim that you will.

Sure, I wish Christian workers wouldn't talk that way. Such talk has clabbered my blood for a generation. But they do. For centuries past they have, and for whatever centuries lie ahead they will continue to. If the day comes that someone says of you, "*This* is of the devil," I admonish you, Chris, check your heart, check your mouth, check your motives. Get clean, get your motives pure, surrender your will, opinions, desires and hopes to the Lord. Then lift up your head to the hills and know that all things are permitted from the hand of the Lord. Sorrow, joy, hope and fear. Refuse to accept *even* this as from the hand of the Lord and chances are you will get bitter. A bitter Christian is a devastated Christian.

The negatives are as much from His hand as the positives.

His work in you will have its share of the bright and dark, the joyful and the sorrowful. He works by means of *all* experiences, and He uses all means to bring us up to the full stature of Jesus Christ.

Your enemy, whoever that ogre is, nonetheless, is a maidservant of Jesus Christ. The Lord is using your enemy, even *His* enemy, to bring you to transformation and His church to triumph.

The highest expression of the love of God is not joy, but suffering, or sorrow, or chastisement. What you thought was rebuke was love most faithful. And what you thought was defeat might have been His victory in your life. Furthermore, what you were quite certain was the enemy himself just might ultimately turn out to be none other than the Lord of life.

Chapter 20

Chris:

Martyrdom is something that has fascinated the Christian church down through the ages. Fox's Book of Martyrs and other such books tell us the wonderful story of those who chose to be burned alive rather than recant their faith, those who stepped in front of a sword to save another's life, those who confessed Christ in the face of certain death, those who laid down their lives rather than curse the name of the Lord. That is all very beautiful, but I would like to be very sacrilegious here and say that martyrdom may not be the highest thing that God might do in a Christian's life.

I look around at the Christians whom I live with, whom I know and love so dearly. They really, truly love Him and would probably die for Him today, even this minute. And if that happens, in awe and reverence we will probably honor them and hallow their memory. But the truth of the matter is I know some of those Christians very, very well. Maybe too well. Some of my Christian friends who would willingly die for Him *today*, and who would probably die gloriously, well . . . they still make terrible roommates . . . and husbands, and wives.

My point? Death by martyrdom is almost the coward's way out.

Suffering. Ah, unlike martyrdom, this can prove to be a mite hard on the soul. It is usually more difficult to live than it is to die. You can look good being a martyr.

(I've always figured, given an arena, a hundred thousand people and a few quick lions, I could put on a show that would be remembered for ages. I just hope the reporters never ask my wife what it was like to live with me.)

Let's say you were somehow saved from martyrdom upon the stake at the very last possible moment. The flame had already scorched your body. Now you are taken to the hospital to recover from severe body burns. I feel certain that in a few days the rest of us would be thinking privately how it might have been better if we hadn't arrived with our water buckets just when we did. You just might be so ornery and despicable a patient, we might wish you had gone ahead and died.

Chris, there are things martyrdom cannot do. Things *only* sorrow can do. Pain can take out of us that which will not yield to the divine by any other means. That which refuses to be replaced by divinity can sometimes be reached only by unjust suffering. The surgeon's scalpel is rarely well replaced by a martyr's scaffold.

Come to peace with this matter, Chris. Out yonder somewhere a great deal of suffering, sorrow and catastrophe almost certainly awaits you.

Chapter 21

Chris:

Every decade of your life has some particular purpose to it. Your twenties are reserved for the purpose of getting saved, consecrating your life wholly and completely to the Lord, and for most of us, finding a Christian mate and marrying. For those doubly blessed of God, perhaps you are brought into a true experience of church life, where there is a fair semblance of balance, where the deep things of Christ are real and valid, and where the church of Christ is pursuing her eternal destiny. As far as your life's relationship to Christ over the long haul is concerned, your thirties will almost certainly be the most significant years of your life. During your thirties you will have to re-evaluate all your commitments, standards and concepts which you formed during your twenties! In fact, you will have to decide whether that consecration of being totally given to Christ which you made in your early twenties is something you really mean to live with the rest of your life. There is a good chance that the 32-year-old man is not willing to live with a commitment he inherited from a 21-year-old boy.

It is in your thirties that you will probably really settle exactly what your relationship will be toward worldliness. You may settle down to one job, one house and a large number of protective buffers that ensure security. You may elect to have a home and children; and for religion you will perform the ancient rite of going inside a church building once or twice a week. Or you may break free of the thirties' security fears, get a mohair tent, grab up your family and set out looking for that city. If something like that happens in your life, and it's in your thirties and not your twenties, then there is a really good chance you will *begin* a genuine relationship with the Lord. (God forbid that you would begin serving Him in your twenties.) It is in your late thirties and through your forties that you will learn to eat dust, desert, wilderness, wasteland, and transverse the northeast corner of hell without even getting thirsty! Here is where true persecution will be faced, where again and again your mettle will be tested. The problems of this period are real: Either depression and disappointment will destroy you or you will learn to live in resurrection. In your fifties you will probably refight some of the battles of your thirties. Some future, huh?

Chris, will you dare to be a free spirit throughout the rest of your life, living for the Lord like a daredevil lives for adventure? In your fifties you will catch that very first feeling of the cold, icy clutches of death beginning to wind his fingers around your outer tent. Either you will elect to run for shelter or you will be overcome with the sense that if you are ever to do anything for the Lord you had better be about the business of getting started. And the fifties just may hold for you your first years of true fruitfulness. And if God is doubly merciful He may even give you a renewal of that longing to know Him deeper. What will happen to you in your sixties (and in your seventies if He permits you to live beyond times appointed)? No one can say, but of this there is a certainty: Until you take your last breath, He will be working to transform you.

Getting old, by the way, is not a guarantee either of

rest from warfare or of transformation. In fact, it could be the bitterest time of your life. That will depend on the reactions which you are right now programming into your life as you deal with the smaller tribulations, pains and struggles of your twenties. When you are 60 and facing disease, financial reverses, disaster, lack of appreciation, treachery, friends becoming enemies, and the never ending loss of all your life's toil and labor, remember, you will be having to live that part of life's battle while standing on a foundation you erected in your twenties!

And if all you have learned in your twenties is no more than simply how to keep from being bitter, then that alone is a miracle worthy to be compared to the parting of the Red Sea. Furthermore, you just might survive your sixties with *that* foundation under your aged feet.

In all of this, may you never give in to security. May you ever be willing to be mobile, follow either cloud or pillar of fire, and may you be found on an upward trail of faith. A faith that says, "He will take care of me until my dying day even if the day I die finds me, at last, with nothing. That is, nothing . . . but Him."

Chapter 22

Chris:

I'll give you a riddle and if you can answer the question for me fully let me know. I have been ministering the Lord for three decades now. It has been a ministry within the walls of church life and a ministry which I hope—and believe—has been centered in the Lord Jesus Christ. But here is my mystery: There are some Christians who have come among us who are *greatly* flawed; they come, listen to the messages, take notes and never miss a meeting; they arrive at every 6 a.m. prayer meeting, read all the good books, do everything exactly as recommended for those who are young in Christ; they pray, sing, testify, wait patiently before the Lord, do everything that Scripture itself admonishes them to do. Yet, they do not change. Why is this? I do not know. But I have noticed something. On a few occasions, I have seen such deeply flawed brothers and sisters, after many, many years of going on unchanged, and sometimes getting away with near murder, I might add, confronted at last. A very peculiar thing happens: More often than not, on the very day they are confronted, they also pack their bags and leave. They may have inflicted years and years of hardship upon the rest of us with their abominable ways (and we did not confront them because their hearts seemed so much for the Lord and we pitied their inability to handle their deep psychological flaws), but once confronted, they ended their sojourn into the deep things of Christ . . . on the spot. This is not always true, of course. But it is true enough to spice our interest in watching the passing parade. I do not know exactly why some people pack and leave when the Lord gets down to bedrock, but somehow, when the Lord got into the neighborhood of their real problems—not surface issues—they left. We came very close to finding out what it was they were holding on to so dearly. So dearly that they didn't want it touched or changed.

I was, of course, speaking of saints who are deeply flawed. But Chris, *all* of us are deeply flawed! You. Me. And that neat, near-perfect Christian sitting next to you.

There are always a few hidden flaws in each of us, flaws so well hidden we don't know we have them. (Usually our brothers and sisters know, though. Isn't that fascinating? We can't see our flaws. Others can. Three cheers for close-knit church life.) Those flaws constitute the major field upon which the battle for our transformation will be fought. I am quick to add that even an all-powerful Lord has a difficult time tearing out some of those well-hidden problems of our lives.

I would like to talk about this a little bit more, for this has troubled me throughout the entire length of my ministry. On several occasions I have gone to a very damaged Christian and asked him to please seek professional help. Sometimes my fellow Christian went off, not to get help but to pout. (Or, in order to maintain his facade of submission to others, he responded and went . . . once.) Remember, I am referring to young believers like yourself who—like you—fervently asked the Lord to transform them at any cost; young Christians who invited the Lord's cross into their lives. The question before the House is this, does such a believer really want help? Does he really wish to be transformed or is he simply enjoying being a Christian and being a part of a people who have given their lives to the Lord? Is he unconsciously enjoying the ministry, the singing, the fellowshipping with Christ in his spirit, yet somehow building a fence around that hidden man, making sure that nothing dear to the self is broken? Is he so weak and lame of soul that he is afraid that if his crutches, his psychological quirks and peculiarities, are challenged he will somehow fall flat on his face, never to recover?

Why is it that many Christians never change, even in some of the most ideal spiritual circumstances ever known?

I do not know the answer, but Chris, I would ask you, are you willing ultimately to be confronted concerning weakness in your life of which you seem to be totally unaware? Whether you are confronted properly or improperly (and I fear in this day and age it will probably be an improper confrontation by an improper person in the midst of an improper work), the fact remains that your *reaction* to that confrontation will speak volumes of the kind of person you really are.

I have to admit that sometimes my heart cheers when I see a cross coming to penetrate that erstwhile Christian, a cross so great that even he cannot escape the change it will work in him. And come it does, invariably.

The old southern spiritual goes:

> It's not my mother nor my brother,
> But it's me, oh Lord,
> Standing in the need of prayer.

It should also say,

> It's not my mother, nor my brother,
> Nor my sister, nor the worker,
> Nor my wife, nor my husband,
> Nor my children
> But it's You, oh Lord,
> Who sent this very uncomfortable problem to me.

There has to be one fact established in you. It just may be central to your going on with the Lord. It is this: Everything that comes into your life is ordered by God. To a Christian nothing is accidental. This includes some awfully, awfully unfair events. Expect to be treated unfairly often.

I'll use a really grizzly example. Let's say you get married. Let's say that about eight years later your wife tells you she is seriously considering a divorce. (Ouch, sorry to use so cruel a thought. I suppose I'm trying very hard to get your attention, Chris.) The looming divorce may not be the Lord's will, but He just might use such extreme circumstances to root out some deep flaw in your makeup. Full possession of your soul is His ultimate goal.

Now, I confess I was reluctant to use such means to get your attention. Let me tell you why. I recall too vividly how many times I've said such things to Christian young people and I watched them walk away hunting under every rock for the work of God in their lives and calling everything that enters their life "the sovereign hand of the Lord to transform me." Be sure we are all willing to accept anything into our lives as *from the Lord, except* those things which can really alter us. Then we forget all about the whole idea of transformation. Sometimes we are momentary atheists, forgetting even that there is a God.

I've watched many young people try to produce a divine work in their lives or hoist some trivial problem to such a high status. The effort is sometimes tragic and sometimes comical but always ludicrous. You can no more imitate what divine life produces in a life than a dog can successfully imitate a man. There is that much discrepancy! I've come, at the end of thirty years of ministry, to realize that the highest revelation delivered concerning the Lord and His ways in not enough to deal with those basic human flaws with which all of us are cursed. Having the highest revealing there is, imitating the highest revelation of His life that man can grasp, turning over every rock in your life and calling it the work of God to transform you, all this is pretty much futile.

At the end of 30 years of working with young people, I have too many vivid memories of 19-, 20- and 21-year-olds fasting, praying, singing, praising, and giving, doing everything and anything they could to make sure God gained ground in them, only to see the most basic flaws remain . . . untouched . . . even fifteen years later.

Chapter 23

Dear Chris:

The work of the cross comes in many different styles, sizes, many different packages and many different colors. It's a rare Christian who truly understands what the cross is in his life. Let me put that another way. It is a rare Christian who can correctly identify the cross as *truly* being the cross once it arrives. Our fallen nature is an absolute genius at keeping the most important part of self's habits from ever going to the cross. Consequently something in us keeps us from seeing the cross even when it is right in front of us. Or, we give the cross a new name, "Unjust, undeserved treatment at the hands of a bunch of buzzards!" Call it that if you wish, but it is, in fact, still the cross, sent by the Lord Himself.

But the cross can come the very opposite way. You can also believe something is the cross when it isn't. For you, it may be that day when you face a Christian friend who tells you, "This is not the cross of Christ in your life; you simply have masochistic tendencies!"

To hear the truth of those devastating words . . . and to *deal* with the truth revealed . . . *that* will be your cross.

Let's look at yet another Christian, one who thinks he is bearing his cross so beautifully. His cross, in his eyes at least, is a bickering, nagging wife. One day he is finally confronted with the truth: "Brother, you are *not* bearing the cross! You are a secretive noncommunicating man who keeps your whole personality hidden away from view. Your wife is not a nagger, she is being driven stark-raving mad by the fact that you have not let her know who you are. You are afraid, you are hidden, in fact, you are downright deceptive. Forbearing with your wife's nagging has absolutely *nothing* to do with the cross nor with what the Lord really wishes to accomplish in your life. On top of everything else, you are super-religious. Your precious cross is a cover-up, a cop-out, a bail-out for the *real* cross that is needed in your life. Your jaw would probably break if you started communicating with your wife. You are safe in your silence . . . the risk and terror and pain would be in talking. You haven't even *started* knowing the cross. On top of everything else, you know virtually *nothing* about true spirituality; you are a super-religious, secretive recluse who is just about to put the finishing touches on driving your wife loony.''

Whew. If that brother, facing truth in stark reality, accepts such an exposure, then he will have allowed the Lord to reveal the true meaning of the cross to his life . . . perhaps for the first time.

For another brother, his day is up when he realizes that his very refined ability to *not* confront someone (but, rather, to bear the cross) is really an act of cowardice. To confront would be his *real* cross.

Conversely, there is the brother who is very proud of the fact that he is frank and outspoken and quick to get things into the light. Somewhere, someday, he will be faced with almost the opposite reality. He is going to have to face up to the fact that there is a cruelness in him, that he is a callous, compassionless man, and for him to *speak* is to refuse the cross. For him to be silent and to accept (as he sees it) injustices would almost kill him. If he manages . . . then the Lord has won a victory.

The wife who thinks that she is the perfect mother and doing such a wonderful job of being the godly wife and mother, may one day have to face the fact that she is, more than anything else, *self-righteous* about her perfection. The brother who constantly, daily pours out his life for others, serving others, who is loved and revered as a true servant of the Lord . . . (we all love him . . . after all, look at all he has done for each of us. *Here*, truly, is a Christian): One day he may have to realize that he is not really serving the Lord but that he is psychologically a very insecure individual and is trying to buy other people's favor by his helpfulness.

Then, there is the sister who is constantly praising the Lord, has given up marriage to serve the Lord full time, is looked upon as one who is truly a disciple of Christ, the picture of the perfect celibate Christian. That woman may one day have to face the stark fact that she is unconsciously a man-hater or is afraid of sex, or has latent homosexual tendencies, and that she has a very low self-image and is trying to buy favor with Christ and with Christians, or unconsciously feels that the Lord was punishing her for being such a nurd. Wow, if she gets caught in this act of self-deception . . . that will be the blackest day of her life. Will she be able to survive? Would she follow Christ if He required her to marry and drop this deception?

I have seen too many Christians who fit the above categories. (You should read what I left out.) When their lives are brought down into shambles in some divine bursts of exposure, truly they taste the full power of the cross for *the first time.* .

As I said, the *true* cross comes in some very surprising packages.

Be sure, when the exposing onslaught of light hits, some Christians prefer to continue the masquerade, steal away in the night and set up their act in the next town.

In fact, when light finally hits "the real you," not one of us wins any medals for gracious acceptance.

None of what I have mentioned here to you may be true; that godly woman who never married may truly be godly. That almost perfect mother may truly be almost perfect. That brother who holds his tongue when he is being damned and gossiped about and lied about may truly be doing the highest thing on earth. All of that may well be true; but in every one of these people, somewhere behind some dark, long-forgotten dungeon door lies a deep, hidden psychological flaw which the Lord is determined to locate, to bring to the light, and to change! That hour may well contain for you more pain than you have ever before experienced. In that hour you will hurt, Chris. There is an excellent chance that you may be very tempted to turn away from the Lord's cross in that moment.

Each of us is carrying around something very precious which we, despite all of our expressions of devotion to the Lord, are not about to give up to the cross. Tragedy of all tragedies . . . we seem never to know this.

As one brother wisely put it, "The cross is usually exactly the opposite of what we thought it was." In the light of all I have said here, is it any surprise God uses sorrow and pain to get through our defenses. What else, pray tell, could penetrate such a bulwark?

Chapter 24

Chris:

A Christian I've known for a long time has, like all of us, a giant fault in him. He has listened to me minister for about seven years. One day we had a serious talk. "Bill," he said, "a long time ago I heard you talk about the cross and I got this idea in my head of a terrible God who causes me to suffer, and that it was good for me to see God that way and to see how unworthy I was. So I've taken everything as from the Lord, afraid He wouldn't love me if I ever denied anything. Look at me, I'm afraid of God, I still work at the same job and the same salary I did seven years ago." Then I get this look that says, "Bill, it's all your fault."

Oh, mercy.

Well, Chris, you won't believe this, but just one hour later I sat down with another Christian. "Well, yes, I've been drinking a lot, and going out with unbelievers. But Bill, remember about seven years ago you said that as Christians we should be well rounded and psychologically balanced? And remember six years ago when you spoke on our being free in Christ? Wow. I was so liberated when I realized I was free to do anything."

Then he gives me this look which seems to say, "When I go before the Lord, if the Lord calls me on my looseness, I'm going to say, 'Bill told me it was all right!'"

Oh, mercy, twice.

Well, Chris, after I staggered home crying and vowing I'd never indulge in public speaking again, I began to reflect on those two conversations. First, both those Christians were trying to make me responsible for their conduct. Secondly, they each heard only that part of the gospel that fit into their natural tendency. And each had a foolproof means of getting away with it. Me!

That's a neat trick. (I wish I could say this scenario had only happened to me once!) What am I saying to you, Chris? For each of those two Christians, the cross was the opposite of what they had assumed it to be. And both had figured out a really neat way to protect their greatest dispositional flaws. They had taken a man-made cross, stamped with my approval, and slipped neatly past the work God had planned to do in them.

What is the cross for me is not the cross for you.[1] What is a great need in your life is no need at all in anyone else's. Yes, the cross will come to you prefitted and custom made. And you *will not like it!* Your blood-curdling screams will probably be heard from here to the gates of heaven. When that well-hidden flaw, which you prized so dearly, the god of your self-life, is at last dragged into the light, oh, pity you. But thank God, the next day will be the beginning of a new era in your life.

Oh, one last thing. Please don't come knock on my door and tell me you read these letters "ten years ago and . . ."

Chapter 25

Chris:

Here is the heart of the matter: You may not have any control over what is happening to you, but you have a great deal of control over your reaction to what is happening to you.

Perhaps one of the most fascinating things that I have observed through my life is how two different people can experience the same tragedy and one will make it a diamond; the other will lose his faith, and even leave the faith. One will yield, the other will rebel. One will work it out, the other will only become bitter.

What was your reaction when your daddy paddled you? It might be an excellent barometer of the reaction that you will have when the Father begins a transforming work in you through the sufferings of this life. Were you rebellious, resentful, antagonistic, bitter, pouty; did you pit rationalization and logic against his actions, did you withdraw? Be careful. You just might lay on God the attitudes that you laid on your dad. You will react to God, when you think He is being unfair, very much the way you do to the fellow who hates your insides and is taking you to court. By the way, how do you react to people who aggressively hate you?

Sometimes He must crack the very fiber of the old ways of your being in order to change you. To come up with new patterns in *old* circumstances is not only difficult, it is sometimes hell. Seeking to handle your

God-induced circumstances from a divine perspective can almost destroy your psychological makeup.

Do you know of what I speak? Then here it is in plain English: When you stop blaming everyone else in creation for your problems and start taking what is happening to you from the hand of God, that can almost drive you crazy. It is one of the most difficult crises of life.

But when, at last, you have finally won a new attitude and a new reaction to your problems, the Lord has also won much ground in your life.

*   *   *   *   *

Stand in a dungeon with me in Vincennes, France. See those cold, dark, muted walls. Know how hot they were in summer and how terribly, frightfully cold they were in winter. See a lone woman standing there, sick, forsaken, forgotten, unjustly imprisoned, yet see heaven etched on her face. Until you have spent more than nine years in Vincennes and the Bastille, you might find it hard to turn to Jeanne Guyon and say: "I have more right to bitterness than you." Look at the pockmarks of a disease that ravaged her beauty. See her health gone, her life work trampled to the ground, her good name branded "heretic." Then see her kiss her Lord's hand and call it His blessed will.

What was happening in the life of Jeanne Guyon? It's very simple. The Lord was cutting away that which He desired be put away. He was making room in her humanity for divinity. He was teaching the human part of her the divine ways of the divine part of her. I need not tell you the legacy that she left to all generations that followed after her. Few women have ever ministered to the body of Christ as did that woman. (Or few men, for that matter.)

She entered in so richly to the fellowship of His sufferings.

* * * * *

It is not the package that suffering comes in. Something different is meted out to each of us. That which would cause absolutely no work of transformation in one Christian's life is an excruciating agony in another's. I'm left only to believe that the suffering that befalls each of us is custom made. It is not the *kind* of affliction that comes to you. At one time or another every one of us seems to cry out: "If it were just something else!" "If it just were not in my head!" "If it were not in my arm." "If it just were not my children." "If it just wasn't my job." Tailor made to do the deepest possible work and at the most inconvenient time, in the most vulnerable spot, *that* bears His fingerprint.

No, it is not what happens to you that is important. How you react to what it is . . . that's important. If your suffering is for Christ, and if your suffering is with Christ, the outcome will depend upon how your spirit faced up to your catastrophe.

For you it may be a wife (if your name were Christine, I'd say "husband" here) who is absolutely unlivable-with. It may be a child who is the discouragement of your life. It may be an illness. It may be a brother who has put himself over you whom you simply cannot abide. It could be any of ten thousand things. Whatever it is, remember that your Lord once knew something quite similar to it.

But remember, there is another experience of His which He has to share with you: an experience He once had with the Father, the experience of having a way made by God to come out on the other side.

Chapter 26

Dear Chris:

Then what of those who are delivered, and delivered instantly, from their sufferings? And what about this matter of exercising faith and therefore being delivered?

Sitting over there near you are two Christians. One is doing great, the other is in great pain; yet, the second seems to be just as worthy as the first. Why do his afflictions persist? Is it a lack of faith? Or because of faith? What a quandary. What are we to believe? Of the two, who is closer to God? Has the afflicted brother failed in faith? Will the proper exercise of faith always triumph over all affliction?

He who has been delivered by his faith has triumphed. He who is not delivered, yet faithfully (though weakly) yields—this one has also triumphed!

And if the truth is known, there is yet a third brother, the one who suffers and yet cannot find the strength to yield gloriously. He is only willing not to become bitter under the strong hand of God. He has no glorious story of healing or yielding, but it may just be that the pain he is going through is great enough and the work of God strong enough to penetrate past all his grumblings and groanings and change the inner man. Maybe, just maybe, even this one has triumphed!

* * * * *

And when you've made peace with your cross, and when you've accepted what the Lord is doing, don't be too quick to be proud of yourself. There is an excellent chance that the heat will only increase. It's really a very rare, rare thing in the annals of Christian history when a saint of God has really truly accepted suffering on the highest possible level. That should comfort you. It does me.

And once he does reach this high estate you would think God would let him off the hook. Well, He doesn't. He just digs deeper, for more gold.

We each *know* what we should do in such hours; we *should* rejoice. But what we should do and what we *can* do are two different things.

"Then what is the good of suffering in my life if I cannot yield, if I cannot surrender, if I cannot come to peace and come to joy with this thing?"

You can do this: You can learn not to become bitter. Chris, that's a *very* big lesson to learn. And a tall order to pull off. Survival alone is considered a great victory, perhaps one of the greatest victories you will ever experience. Would to God more Christians would taste *that* victory.

* * * * *

Just because you are afflicted, it does not necessarily fall out that what happens to you will work into you an eternal weight of glory. There is an inner chamber within you that must in some way be rightly related to that affliction. Your inner being somehow must give acquiescence.

How can an internal relationship be so important to an external problem? The answer to that is simple:

There is nothing that will ever come to you, no matter where it comes from, that can truly damage you, unless you receive it with a wrong attitude. Pain might be there, yes, and the thing might ultimately end up causing your death, true. Nonetheless, that inflicted injury cannot harm the inner man unless you have a wrong attitude toward the injury. If the attitude is correct, that injury simply cannot destroy you.

Everything—excepting sin—that comes to you, comes from the Lord's hand. Every tragedy has an ultimate good to it, *unless* you allow that tragedy to separate you from the Lord.

What happens to you is usually beyond your control, but how you receive it, your attitude toward it, ah! *that* is a different matter.

> The eternal essence of a catastrophe
> Is not the tragedy itself,
> But your reaction to it.

* * * * *

When the storm is over, when the ravaging destruction has ceased, and you look about you and know you have failed . . . you *know* you didn't reach God's highest in this episode of suffering . . . and you wonder what was the good of it . . . Remember, if nothing else, you may just be a little bit more humble.

That, too, is quite a victory.

If it comes about that (1) bitterness cannot reach you, *no matter what befalls you*, and (2) if He has brought an ounce of humility into you (by humiliating you with yet one more failure) . . . then He is well on His way to having revolutionized your life.

If you pass through these two obstacle courses, as left-handed as the accomplishment may seem, suffering will have done its work, and done it well.

I had this statement framed and hung over my desk. I wish every Christian could have it seared upon his mind.

> The whole exercise of blame and resentment is a waste of time, accomplishing nothing. No matter how much fault you find in another person, nor the amount of blame you charge him with, it is not going to change *you*.
>
> The only thing you accomplish in such an exercise is to keep the spotlight off you. Looking for an external reason for what is going on inside you is to miss the point. You may succeed in making someone else feel guilty, true; and you may discharge a lot of negative emotions, true; but you will not succeed in changing whatever it is about your innate disposition that is making you unhappy.

Chapter 27

Dear Chris:

There is a misunderstanding about church life that seems to be innate to our nature. In fact, there is a misunderstanding even about God which seems to be innate to our nature. It is this: We see the times of rejoicing and blessing as times when the Lord is with us and is pleased with us. The times of difficulty, on the other hand, signal that we have done something very, very wrong, and the blessing of the Lord is not with us. This attitude seems even more prevalent when it occurs in an experience of church life.

I have observed through the years that most Christians have little understanding of the word "season." Our Lord is a seasonal God: He comes, He departs. His faithfulness never changes, but His seasons do! There are seasons when the tree is green, there are seasons when it is dry, and seasons when, for the life of us, the thing looks dead. Now, does this mean you are serving some capricious God who comes and goes by whim? Or could it be, Chris, that it is only through *seasons* that true growth may come?

During the span of the generation that I have been ministering to God's people I have yet to find a Christian but what he has hit a long run of what could be called bad luck. Invariably he begins to entertain the thought that either God has left him *or* that somebody lied to him about what God was like . . . "I never heard anyone tell me God allows things like this to happen."

Listen, Chris, it was not Santa Claus who redeemed you and won you to himself; it was a suffering God who had known pain and death long before He created the first molecule.

Paul said, "Does not nature teach us?" Fruit from a tree comes to us as a result of three or four seasons.

A church cannot always be up. A people who try to ever be in an upward state of rejoicing will one day have a lot of catching up to do on the down side. An always "up" church is in for some of the most *positive* nervous breakdowns the world has ever seen.

The Christian *and* the Lord's body both need rain and sunshine, cold and hot, wind and doldrums. Seasons of joy, seasons of sorrow, times when the Lord is so real it seems any activity you undertake is a spiritual experience. Seasons of dryness, when things are so bleak that even a plateful of Sinai sand would be considered a feast!

And are not these seasons from the hand of God? If so, what is His goal in the matter? He is taking you to that place where you can be a man for all seasons. Where seasons don't faze you . . . no, not even the glorious ones. An old apostle said it so well to a young man, "Be ready in season, be ready out of season."

* * * * *

If you cannot handle the seasons, if you end up moaning and groaning; if you end up being frustrated, writhing in self-pity or just generally angry, or if you end up packing your bags because the dry spell seems so long, so hopelessly permanent, the seasons of joy so few, so short, so shallow; then, dear brother, it was good that this fact about your heart was made known. The heart *will* eventually reveal itself, you know.

* * * * *

You need seasons. You will need to overcome the season of joy. If you are addicted to joy, then that addiction will have to be broken. And if sorrow and dryness lay you out flat, then you're going to have to be broken of that luxury, too. And if you are the fellow who is always parched dry even when the water of God is waist deep, then surely you need some radical rearranging in your psychological makeup.

The day must come when every season is taken fairly much the same. That is, you can go forward regardless.

Chris, you will *not* lay hold of these matters in your twenties, so go ahead and shout yourself hoarse in wet seasons and cry yourself hoarse in dry ones. Leave the better 95% of transformation to your Lord. We are all very subject to seasons; yet those seasons are there to make us eventually seasonless. There is only one way you are ever going to learn to triumph over all seasons, and that is to go through each and every season . . . many times. When you can reckon the sound of abundance of rain and the hot blowing wind of a dry spell exactly the same, then, Chris, you will be nearing the land of maturity.

So please, never say—when you are utterly lost out there in the midst of some hot blowing sandstorm—that you were not warned. Such sandstorms are also the ways of God.

Chapter 28

Dear Chris:

Thanks for telling me about the Christians with whom you meet. Chris, do you realize that in any gathering of believers, everyone who comes there comes with mixed motives? Consciously or unconsciously, virtually everything we do has a double motive to it. (Let's only hope the godly motive is the one that wins out.) Anyway the doubleness of our motives must be burned out. That takes a great deal of time. Most of us in our twenties can't even find the dark motives of our hearts and, consequently, don't really believe they are there. In your thirties you may have times when you can't see anything but your double motives and wonder if there is anything else in you. Right now only the Lord knows what those motives are. You are unaware of them, and so is everyone else. So much ambition, so much human strength, so much uncrucified, undealt-with fleshliness...and selfness. How little inner expansion of the spirit. The Lord has such a great work to do among the people with whom you now live and gather. It seems sometimes the fire will burn up everything before He burns out our dross. What a *small* nugget of gold it is which we find in the holocaust of ashes and embers.

It will be only after a titanic breaking that you will, in one ghastly moment, catch sight of the true motives of your own heart. It's going to take a lifetime, *your* lifetime, for the Lord to disillusion you in the vaunted trust you now have in your own self. There is no such thing as a man who does not have an inordinately high view of himself, including the person suffering from a tragic—and genuine—case of low self esteem.

Chris, if you are one of those who hides from this fact of life, if you get behind a facade that announces humbly that you have no trust in yourself, then you are probably trying to cover up just how deep and dark an ambition really does lurk within you. You may be afraid the monster might be found and paraded in the village square, to your shame. And so the Christian grovels in his self-distrust. Gee, when I look back on the last 30 years and see how mixed and how very complex each and every one of us is, I wonder at the genius of a God who can yet transform us into something whole.

* * * * *

Someday you will marry. I hope you will still be in "body life" then, too. There is nothing that requires more humility than a marriage. Within that marriage there will probably never be a moment quite as humbling as the moment when you and your spouse call for help. (That hour will almost surely arrive.) Fact is, most of us are so proud we either refuse help or wait so long that we have waited well nigh *too* long. On that black day the two of you will have things so royally fouled up that you are going to need far more than a referee. You will need someone who will be able to penetrate the deepest, most remote, and most hidden part of your motives, your nature, your disposition . . . your very wellsprings.

And if you get really good help, you are going to scream, at least inwardly, at being so unkindly exposed.

124

And in that moment when the dam breaks and all the problems and hurts and hostilities break loose, there is an excellent chance your marriage will be driven to the very brink of destruction.

So be it. And when it is brought back from destruction, as it inevitably will be, your marriage will rest on a far firmer and far more realistic foundation than the cotton candy and spice foundation upon which it had been originally grounded. The Lord will have gained in you that which cannot be gained in any other way but by working through home and marriage crises.

When the horror of it is over, you might take a moment to look in the mirror carefully. You might see upon your brow the first faint brush strokes of maturity and, who knows, maybe humility or compassion.

On the other hand, if, in those dark days, you rebel, refuse all help, refuse to yield, then a great deal of the Lord's investment in you will be lost. There is no grander hour in the life of a Christian than when he renders up his sword. How does the song read?

> Help me to render up my sword
> That I might conqueror be.

* * * * *

In that dark hour when everything seems to have fallen apart and you are mystified at what is going on in your life, remember that your stress has its counterpart in God. He may not be worried, but He is very concerned about what is going on in you. He is looking to do a replacement: something of you taken out, something of His Son put in the empty place. If you are in a circumstance that is extremely perplexing (let's say a health problem that defies all the rules of healing) if you are surrounded by people at work or in your home or in your fellowship who simply cannot understand you, the truth is, you are probably having some long-forgotten prayer answered. It was a foolish prayer that *you* foolishly prayed, "Lord, conform me to Your image. Apply the cross to the dark side of me. Expose the hidden things even I cannot see. Lord I desire to be wholly Yours."

What can ease the heartache? Probably nothing. But if something can, it is possibly this: to realize in your deepest part that this mess came from His hand.

* * * * *

What can you do, in your hour of hurting, that might please your Lord? Be careful. This is a dynamite question! The hyper-religious person can make a life's career or a mental ward out of a question like that! So, my guarded answer is: very little.

You can rejoice. That's one possibility. You can yield to Him. With joy you can offer up to Him the situation and say, "Lord, I know this is from Your hand."

But the chances are you are not going to get anywhere near that. So what can you do in the midst of adversity? You can kneel; you can weep, and weep, and weep. *This* you can do.

There is one thing you must not do. Complain if you must, groan if you must, and get angry if you must. But oh, dear brother, stay far distant from bitterness and from blaming others. No matter what it is, don't blame others. Do that and you are dangerously close to forfeiting all future spiritual growth.

You may feel strongly you do not deserve this deluxe disaster that has befallen you, but try to remember the man Joseph. He didn't deserve what happened to him, either. Nonetheless, though he saw the evil which men had done, he saw the good which God was doing.

* * * * *

I'd like to close this pile of letters and notes with a very personal word to you on a subject very dear to my heart, or I should say, a subject that burdens my heart.

Chris, I do not see anything that is going to be taking place in the first ten years of your Christian life which will bring you to where your spirit is in control of your soul. I do not think that reading what is written here and going out and faking things you have grasped intellectually will be of any great help to you.

I wish I could address these same words to young workers who begin leading little home groups, start calling those things "church life" and teaching elemental truths of the Christian walk.

There is always the danger, if you have not grown up your entire Christian life in a moderated non-fanatical experience of church life, that that which you are calling your spirit is really nothing more than a distorted soul.

Time, plus the cross. Plus church life. Plus a lot more time. Then throw in a great deal of personal, first-hand encounter with Christ. Stir. Then some more time, and a lot more of the cross working on your positive nature and your negative nature. Eventually the spirit will gain the upper hand.

* * * * *

Is it possible to know if there is true brokenness in

a man? I think so. Such a man is not in rebellion toward anything: (1) nothing in his circumstances, (2) nothing that has to do with what other men inflict upon him, (3) and certainly not anything that God chooses to lay within his life. He is at peace in all three circumstances. Chris, no man is going to arrive at such a walk unless, like a grain of wheat, he has fallen into the ground and died.

What happens to that seed within the earth is a pretty good picture of what awaits you. The husk of the seed breaks; after the breaking a life deep within comes seeping through. But it is only when that outer shell *is buried in darkness* that the inner man begins to seep up and outward through cracks that were brought on through death and crushing.

Chapter 29

Dear Chris:

You know that Jesus Christ was perfected through suffering even though He was perfect. What does that mean? Think about it.

There are things the Son of God did not know as a human being. Before the incarnation He knew all things as the eternal Son within the Holy Trinity. But some things He did not know, not experientially, once He was sheltered inside a human body. The human life part of Jesus Christ had not learned (at least not experientially) that obedience is learned only through pain. (The divine portion of the Son of God had learned that *before* creation.)

Now, if the Son of God learns obedience—be it the human part of him or the divine part—only through pain, and He is perfect, and He is very God of very God, then will you and I, frail and fallen creatures that we are, will we learn obedience through unending prosperity, uninterrupted bliss, blessing and joy?

* * * * *

Be grateful, Chris, that both the divinity of Jesus Christ has suffered and the humanity of Jesus Christ has suffered. Jesus Christ knows what it means to hurt. He knows what it means to have pain coursing through the heart and stabbing at the body. If he did not know that, the church would have an ill-equipped God to be the Lord of our assembling.

Now, if the sons of God are perfected through suffering just as the Savior was perfected through suffering, then it follows that there is an ingredient absolutely essential to the Christian life. Without it, there is incompletion.

* * * * *

Can you see Christ suffering while on earth? And can you see that suffering daily maturing Him?

Today there is the Christ-ness about your God—something He gained here on earth—which must be worked into you. Can that which *is* Christ, that which matured Him, brought Him to fullness and is now part of Him, can *that* portion of Him be brought into your life? Yes. But not apart from suffering. There is something very self-centered in you, and in me, that will never die except through the jabbing pains of adversity.

If you evade, if you resist, if you hold on to that deep self-centered place, guarding it in such a way that it cannot be reached, even by the hand of God, then there will remain in you something unchanged and unbroken throughout all the rest of your life. An altar, a throne room, an inner sanctuary where self is worshipped will never be cast down. Unbridled, unrestrained pain sometimes serves as a battering ram to break down the door that leads to that super-hidden, sacrosanct room. Pain can be very irreligious and downright unthoughtful about the places it chooses to barge into.

So, be sure, one day the Lord will lift the hand of protection from you. Out of love He will say, "Now,

I will allow this one to suffer." And so, you will begin to fellowship with Christ in His suffering. Suffering had purpose in Him. And suffering has purpose in you.

* * * * *

Someone has made a most awesome statement: "It seems that sometimes our faith cannot be perfected until that moment comes when it appears the Lord has denied us."

There are worse things than mystery and question that can befall you. A few believers touch even the very vortex of the cross: He takes them to the cross, as He did His Son and there He utterly forsakes them.

The question screams for an answer. *Why?* I for one do not know.

Sometimes it seems the Lord must appear to forsake us to accomplish His work in us. There will possibly even be moments when the Lord seems to be faithless. If that troubles you, then remember Abraham—his faith was brought to the very cliff's edge of rational belief. And if that is not enough, Chris, remember your Lord.

Chapter 30

Chris:

When I first began these notes to you, I observed that there are people who view the Christian life as one endless joy ride, while others see it as a lifetime of miseries. At this point in our correspondence, I am just a little concerned that I may appear to belong to the second group.

Not so. I've lived one very exciting, hair-raising Christian life. Yet, I must honestly confess my scroll has been charged with its share of earthly pain. Nonetheless, as I look back, I can still say, "It's been fun. Sometimes it's been downright awesome."

Why, then, I ask myself, have I run the risk of leaving the impression with my nephew that the Christian life is just two floors up from the torture chamber? (Such is the occupational hazard, it seems, of all men who write and speak on the subject of the cross.) Frankly, I'm not sure, but looking back on my experiences in this matter I will venture one possibility. It has to do with some vivid memories which come to my mind and which, quite honestly, still haunt me. I have witnessed some really heartbreaking results that have come out of the lives of dear Christians whose lives—having once been touched with pain—were completely shattered. They were not able to handle the idea that as Christians, they might be called on to suffer.

Chris, for two decades now the cross has had a major place in all my spoken ministry. None can charge me with not having dealt with suffering in the Christian life, nor of failing to warn young believers of the rough waters ahead.

But wait. I better rephrase that statement: I would not *expect* anyone to say, "Bill, you never warned me the journey could get *this* rough." As you may guess, I do hear just such statements!

Funny, but once a Christian begins to hurt, he seems to come down with amnesia, forgetting he ever heard of such things as the cross and suffering. And in those moments when the ship enters its first really rough sea, some Christians elect to depart the whole Christian venture.

I recall having once inquired of the state of a young couple very dear to me, but whom I had not heard from in some time, only to be told that they had more or less left the Lord's way, giving as their reason that they "couldn't understand why God had allowed all this to happen to us." In inquiring as to what "all this" was, I discovered the reasons to be amazingly trivial. At least, I know a number of Christians who are still going on with Him who would have gladly exchanged problems with them.

In my lifetime, I have seen—as a few examples—the following: A Christian beginning to lose his faith because he had to live in a crowded apartment for two weeks; another because he didn't have a job for one week; another because he couldn't pay a month's rent; another because he had a question no one could answer; another for being misquoted; another for being ignored (or was it overlooked?); another for having a case of the flu he couldn't shake by the end of two months. For these things, men and women would almost lose their faith?

My point is this: Such memories cause me to try, ever so valiantly, to get the attention of the new Christian, telling him in every way I know, that he must inevitably encounter a deluge of sorrows. I fail at that task all too often, leaving the young Christian still unaware of what is ahead; and, at the same time, he picks up the distinct impression that the Christian venture is but one long, miserable study in sadness.

Rather paradoxical, isn't it?

In the light of all this, I have a very personal word for you, my dear young nephew. If such small sufferings as I have just recounted can sink your Christian ship, let me assure you that there are several thousand crises out there waiting for you that are big enough to sink the entire British navy! As a Christian worker, I know of no truth that can be told you, no "deeper life" experience available to you, no hand of help which can be extended to you that will keep your frail ship afloat. The *only* thing I know to do is to move back and give you plenty of room in which to sink!

I never stop being amazed at our amazement at being called on to suffer. I join with Peter, "Don't be so surprised when these trials hit."

I would like to add a positive word here, Chris. I do have other memories! I have watched some of God's people, whose lives have been charted through some of the worst storms life can produce, come through these trials with all flags (eventually) flying and all guns (eventually) blazing! It is *these* memories which cheer me on and keep the cross central in life and ministry.

Then why do some of us sink so easily? There must be a thousand different reasons. I will point to one: We imagine one kind of trial, romanticize it, prepare for it, and think we see it coming only to get smashed flat by a trial so completely different from anything we ever dreamed.

Chris, I hope for you a beautiful, full and exciting Christian life. In the meantime, I recommend you not only expect the best, but also prepare for the worst! When you are old, when you come to the end of this fantastic, fascinating pilgrimage, and when you pause for a moment to look back, I've a notion you will conclude that you received the outer limits of both!

I implore you, Chris, let nothing that enters your life ever deter you from the upward call.

Your brother in Christ,
Bill

P.S. I think it is time now that we turn our attention a little more to the matters of suffering and of transformation as it relates to you *within* a practical experience of the body of Christ.

Part III

Chapter 31

Chris:

I've never been in the gathering you are part of there in Portland. I'm glad you are in an informal fellowship. If you are in a genuine and practical experience of church life, there will be help available to you and help given to you. I've been part of such informal meetings—perhaps *primitive* is a better word—for nearly 20 years.

I'm also glad you are in an experience of church life because what I say will make more sense to you. It is difficult to understand the true purpose of suffering outside an experience of body life. Why man suffers isn't a difficult question to deal with if you see it from God's viewpoint and not your own. You have to see that your Lord created with a purpose, and the end result of that purpose is primarily for Him. He is, right now, working toward fulfilling *His* purpose in having created.

* * * * *

Chris, if you ever joined yourself to a close-knit community of believers . . . Wait, let me stop right there; I am *not* speaking of walking into a large auditorium of gothic design—erroneously referred to as a church. I speak, rather, of the daily experience of church life—of Christians daily and intimately sharing their lives with each other in a positive experience of the church. As I was saying, if you get involved in *church life* then eventually you will be struck with a rather unnerving fact: There is a vast amount of suffering going on in the lives of the Christians you are with. The longer you live in church life and the more you live intimately with other believers, the more you will see the enormity of the suffering of those around you. Eventually, you begin to think you must be living with the most unlucky people on earth. You may even wonder if you are in a group that is under some sort of curse. You wonder if God isn't trying to tell the lot of you He really isn't with you.

Why so much suffering among Christians?

When you first get saved, you have the idea that the Christian life is going to be one great, glorious festival. Later, at least in church life, you pause to look around, only to find suffering, not blessing, abounding.

One reason that an experience of church life seems so plagued with hard luck is that you have an exceptionally accurate vantage point. Now, if—instead of being in the church—you were living in a nice suburban home down at the end of a cul-de-sac with, say, four close friends, you would never realize the broad expanse of suffering the human race was enduring. Instead, you would only be thinking, "I've got four of the unluckiest friends who ever lived." Increase the circle of your intimate relations to, say, 50 people, *then* you have a bird's eye view of human society. And of human agony. Fifty people—closely watched—can tell you the story of the human race.

Four friends can't; church life will.

This experience we call church life (for want of a better term) sometimes takes on the appearance of a battlefield holocaust. Keep a steady heart as you get your first understanding of how deeply the Fall has damaged mankind. Keep a steady head as you begin to see the vastness of the suffering which is meted out to each of us. That fellowship of Christians you are with may *not* be under a curse. There is a very good chance that all those serene looking folks living down at the end of that tranquil little cul-de-sac are also going through their own private little hells. I trust I will not shock you, Chris, if I tell you that things are bad all over!

The fate which has been meted out to you, cruel as it may appear, is no more than the average lot bestowed upon almost every one of us earth-bound pilgrims. That very simple fact rarely shows itself in clear detail, and learning it first-hand can stagger the best among us.

There is a difference, nonetheless, between you and the typical family living in one of those faceless housing developments. The Christian who has totally yielded himself to Christ suffers in life somewhat differently from the unbeliever. (He also suffers differently from the not-so-committed Christian.) Why? Because such a Christian is suffering the Lord's sufferings. He has embraced the anguish that is deep inside the Lord Himself. Touch that burning flame and you are altered. Changed. Such an encounter *cannot* but alter you.

When a Christian, any Christian, decides to give his life utterly and totally to Jesus Christ without reservation, abandoning the world, giving up security, turning to simplicity and heading for the deep things of God, that is, the things nearest and dearest to the Lord; you can be sure that soon thereafter he is going to touch some portion of pain. When he does, he has commenced his inevitable journey down the road of suffering. That pilgrimage will carry him from glory to glory, until one day, by the sovereign hand of the Lord, he is made into something not altogether unlike *Him.* Conformed to *His* image. *Mostly* by suffering.

Why are so many of the Christians around you going through such deep floods and fiery flames? Because it is their destiny. Give *your* life that completely to Christ, brother Chris, and it will be your destiny, too.

* * * * *

I have been close to a group of Christian young people, about 100, for over a decade now. I know with certainty that each and every one of them has been warned: "Give your life utterly to Christ and you will eventually suffer much more than you can now comprehend." But there is no way a man can communicate to daring young Christians the amount of suffering they will encounter in one lifetime. Again and again they have been cautioned, in every way known. Yet, each time that sovereign hand of God has fallen on one of them and he (or she) has truly entered into the fellowship of Christ's sufferings, he is always surprised how hard, how unbearable, is the cross.

I expressed these very words to these young Christains when they were in their early twenties, only a few months after their conversion. For better or worse, they did not have the good sense to run out the door. These were young Christians who loved the Lord, who would not be stopped, not even by the cross. Nonetheless, in every single case, by the time they reached their mid-thirties each and all had encountered that special furnace reserved only for the Christian who has abandoned himself to Christ.

If you consecrate your life, setting it apart to Jesus Christ, then suffering will certainly be a good part of your earthly lot.

Chris, if you come this way, don't waste one moment of that suffering. Look up! See the pain that is inside of Him! The pain you know in the moment of suffering was bequeathed to you so that, except for His being the sin bearer, you might touch everything He has known and experienced.

* * * * *

There is a sense in which a believer never knows suffering that is original. The suffering which you experience is not really yours. Rather, you have but touched an experience of suffering which Jesus Christ has already gone through.

Have you ever been persecuted for being a Christian? Did that experience of persecution almost destroy you? Did agony compound agony? Certainly your experience was neither original nor unique. Though you knew exquisite agony, what really happened was you drank from Jesus Christ's own cup of suffering.

On the day of your conversion you became a partaker of Him. In partaking of Him you have also partaken of His experiences. Any pain you have known was nothing more than the experience of touching His pain. In that moment you knew something of what He went through; what He went through became experiential in your life.

Have you known sorrow? Sorrow so great, so unutterable that you found it difficult even to breathe? Then you have known, for one brief moment, the deep grief and the inner heavings of the Son of God.

He has a storehouse of His sufferings. You have but partaken of something therein.

You have had fellowship with Jesus Christ, have you not? You have touched His joy, I believe. Did you complain about experiencing His joy? One day you fellowshipped with Him in the great joy of salvation. Did you complain that day?

Someday you must have yet another fellowship, an experience common to you and the Lord. You must touch the fellowship of His sufferings. Yes, you must taste that fellowship, too. After all, it was His. Just as that first ecstatic touch of joy which you had was, in fact, first known by Him, so, too, the suffering which you refer to as "your suffering" was actually first His. The suffering you are having right now, it is His, as He knew it, passed on to you. You are fellowshipping with Him in what He has already known.

* * * * *

An ancient prophet told us, "He bore our griefs."

What does that mean to you, brother Chris? For Jesus Christ suffered, suffered that which divinity alone must suffer; but He also suffered things *in your place*.

Now, Chris, you have the opportunity (and privilege) of standing in that very same position. *You* may bear some of *His* sorrow, some of His pain, some of His suffering, yes, and perhaps a little of His agony. If you do, several things will happen.

You will spare Christ of suffering . . . sufferings that come to Him out of a lack that exists in the body of Christ.

Somehow, unknown to you, you will later spare some

other pilgrim a portion of suffering which was originally meant for him. Furthermore, just as you will never know what it means, "He bore *my* griefs," someone else will never know that you spared them great pain.

* * * * *

I have watched a group of young people who were called and who responded to that call, who utterly consecrated their lives to Christ. I have watched the drama which thereafter unfolded. I have seen the tension heighten. I have seen the pain become more intense and less bearable with every passing year.

On some future day those dear men and women (for they are not so young now) will stand in a living room somewhere before a group of young people. They will make the same declaration which was made to them about suffering and about the cross. But that next generation of young saints will not be stopped. They will dare, against all good judgement, to follow Christ, utterly. I have a prayer for that second group of young people. My prayer is that there will be a number of survivors from the first group who will be there—be there to help, to strengthen, to counsel and to confront when flame and flood arrive on the scene. In that hour those men and women who are now no longer young will be able to lend their strength—won in fire—to that second generation who will then no longer be ignorant.

It is so important that the dark inner realms of suffering be touched by older saints in church life . . . for the sake of the young. You understand that. Well, it was just as important that *He* be the first to touch that dark realm so that *He* could later care for others—so that, even later, *they* could care for you.

Among us the suffering of Christ abounds.
II Corinthians 1:5

* * * * *

What was it that Christ suffered?

I remind you, we will know no suffering, no pain in this life as believers, but what He had the experience first. We cannot go beyond His suffering. So let us ponder this tear-stained question, "What was it Christ suffered?"

You are *in* Christ. That is a fact you may not yet have fully grasped experientially. That doesn't matter. God has. When the Lord looks at you, He sees you *in* Christ. He sees you one with Christ, part of the very being of Christ. These things are mysteries; though so certainly given to us, yet they are not clearly understood by frail mortals such as we. But of this you can be certain: Everything which happened to Him who is the Christ, these same things happen to the members of the body of Christ. His experience is destined to be the experience of the church.

> Did He suffer?
> Then it follows
> As the night follows day
> You shall suffer.
> Did He die?
> Then you also die.
> Did He rise?
> Then you also rise.

Yes, it is true that all these experiences that Christ has had are present and accomplished facts. Yes, I *have* been crucified. Yes, I *have* died in Christ. I have *already* risen *in* Christ. But I *shall* also enter into and partake of some small portion of His suffering while I live upon this clod. I shall, experientially, touch His sufferings. Paul did. Peter did. So will you. So do I. And while she is still confined to this earthen ball, still locked in time and confined to visible realms, the experience of the bride will follow hard upon that experience which was His own.

It was the Roman Catholics' belief, during the middle ages, that only a few very special people could attain to the high places of sainthood. It was their belief that a special catastrophic loss, sorrow, or pain was destined for a certain few who would in turn be specially used in the kingdom of God. Is that true, or is it, rather, possible for any yielded heart to know Him well? There is nothing in the writings of the first century that indicate that there is a special breed of people for anything.

What the Lord is doing in your life is toward this end: to make you as complete in Christ as any other saint who has ever lived. He is working the same thing in me. He has fashioned every circumstance that enters into your life toward that end. There are no accidental happenings in any Christian's life.

His goal is to change you into His likeness.

You, as one lone individual, cannot be changed into the *completeness* of *all* that Christ is. The all-encompassing Christ is simply too great for you to express. But you can express some part of His life. With that fact we come face to face with the purpose of the church. You cannot express all of Christ. Neither can the brother sitting next to you. Yet the Lord is seeking transformation in both. Look around. The same thing is happening to every person in that room. Not a single one of them can express all of Christ. But Chris! Each one of you *can* express some unique part of Christ! Then look what happens when you gather in one of those informal meetings. Assembled together in that room are all the riches that are Christ. And those riches can be seen *and* heard!

In my judgment that is one of the most wondrous facts in the universe.

Chapter 32

Dear Chris:

As I mentioned to you earlier, I have worked with a group of Christian young people for over a decade. I had a front row seat watching them grow up. They gave their hearts and lives to seeing the life of the church restored. They set out for something practical and experiential. In the early days of their venture, they lived in the midst of a great deal of light and revelation *and* a great deal of very *real, daily* experience of touching Christ. Most of what they experienced were things that had been restored somewhere else along the way in centuries previous to their own. Be that as it may, what those young people had was rare. Now they have experienced what few Christians in our century have ever experienced, and perhaps now some of them will go after those things which no Christians in any century (save one) have ever known. They had to start at zero . . . move from there to things rare, yet restored. In the beginning, nothing had been experienced except salvation. Their task was simple: to find out what had been restored and experience it. They had to somehow lay hold of those things and then keep on holding on to them! Then they marched off the map. Some of them are determined to bring back again to living reality things lost for two millenniums.

Chris, awesome events had to take place in the lives of that group of young people (whose average age at the start was about 21). The Holy Spirit had to invest an abundant amount of time and energy in those lives. I repeat, they were starting off at ground zero. Restoration starting at ground zero does not have the most encouraging prospects of success.

Some would become disconsolate. Therefore somebody had to comfort. But who would be the first to comfort? Why, the first to suffer! Who would be the first to speak of the cross with great power and great conviction? (That is, who would be able to speak of the cross with words firmly set in reality?) Who would be the first to declare resurrection? Only one who had died! Who would comfort, except the comforted? Who would heal, except the healed? Who would wield power? None, except those who had been made terribly weak. Who would shield us from legalism and law, except he who had had that beast broken in the depths of his very own nature? Who would pour out his life in long hours of counseling, guidance, direction, except the one who had gained a great deal of counsel, guidance, and direction...slowly, painfully, richly.

So you see, it was given to that group of young men and women to drink very, very deeply of a cup of which they had theretofore never sipped. Some of the wine they sipped was restored wine, and some of it was new wine, but for that little band of believers *it was all new!* Not one drop of that wine did they ever sip except by experience. And in spiritual experience there must be suffering.

Now you know, dear Chris, why it is the Lord has told us:

> You suffer
> For the sake
> Of the whole body.

If some brother in that group of believers had not suffered, then that entire group of believers would have had absolutely nothing.

It is necessary for you to suffer—for the body's sake. There is no church, there is no experience of restoration, there is no laying hold of those things which have been lost, unless someone, very possibly *you*, suffers.

No suffering, no restoration.

The riches which we have today have come to us because someone before *us* suffered, and that "someone" gave to the body what had been restored out of that suffering.

I have spoken personally and intimately, but what I have said to you about our experience is really nothing more than the record of the first century church. Back in those days, too, someone went through all the experiences you read about, and then they shared them with others. Those, in turn, passed their experiences on to still others.

Let me put it another way. The apostles stood before One who had touched absolutely all spiritual realms, One who had laid hold of all blessings and *all* sufferings and all graces. One day these apostles went into a large city. There, for about seven years, they lived in the midst of thousands of new Christians. On that day called Pentecost, their lives were *already* rich. They had a great deal to share with others. Then, as the years unfolded, the brothers and sisters with whom they lived now shared in and drank fully and experientially of all that those twelve had experienced. Those Christians took what the apostles had experienced, turned, and gave it to a new crowd of young believers who were waiting out there in great need.

So you see, Jesus Christ experienced suffering, and

what He won out of that suffering He passed on to the apostles. How? By allowing them to know *His* sufferings. They gained so much by partaking of His suffering. What they gained they passed on to a vast multitude of new Christians. And how did *those* Christians gain what the apostles had? By fellowship in the sufferings of Christ. And the riches they gained from that suffering they passed on to the rest of the body of Christ. And so it has been for 2,000 years.

Once I witnessed a group of young people who saw this, and they—but wait. What about you? Now, Chris, you suffer. Why?

Well, at least one reason is evident. You suffer for the sake of the body.

* * * * *

Perhaps we should place this sign on the wall somewhere in our homes:

> Church life may be
> hazardous to your health.

And the statement *is* true! But, oh, your loss can be so healing to His body.

Chapter 33

Dear Chris:

It is difficult for either an individual—or a group—to be persecuted without lashing back. Maybe that is why persecution is one of God's favorite handmaidens. It gets down to basics. It is difficult, is it not, to suffer wrong from those who deliberately cast you into the worst light? If there is anything that will provoke an otherwise "perfect" Christian to do or say something un-Christian, it is unjust persecution. (By the way, Chris, if you think your enemies will be impressed with your godly silence, don't. They won't even notice it. And the people who hear them slander you and believe what they hear won't notice either.)

It is almost impossible to keep love in your heart when you see Christian friends in prison. Or killed. And yet your God permits these inequities. Oh, what a triumph it is when even one Christian can go through all of that hurt without becoming cynical or bitter.

But why does God permit such suffering to befall His bride?

This suffering produces gold in the lives of those individuals who suffer. That gold, in each life, is then blended into the body of Christ to make the bride what she ought to be.

Careful, Chris, the very thing that you are now rebelling against just might be in perfect harmony with the Lord. What you see and feel so painfully may be the Lord's effort to polish a stone.

Greatly rejoice.
Right now you must suffer a little bit.
But these sufferings
These tests of your faith
Are worth a great deal more than gold.

Survive this
And your faith will be proven genuine.
And the result will be praise and glory and honor.

1 Peter 1:6-7

* * * * *

Can you, perhaps, appreciate why the Lord dispenses seasons of sufferings into your life? There will come an hour when the bride of Christ will be in very great need; and in that hour of the crunch it is crucially important that *you* will have *already* known how to bear that particular suffering—suffering which everyone else is touching for perhaps the first time. They will need *you*.

Now turn around. Despite the fact that you are very young, can you see coming behind you a new throng of believers? They are just beginning. They are at zero. For them everything they touch of the Christian life will be completely new. Do you see them? They will arrive on the scene at perhaps any moment. But before they arrive, someone *must* suffer for their sake.

It has been given to you,
Not only to believe on Him,
But also to suffer for *His* sake.

* * * * *

One day you are going to look back over your life to

recall to mind many an incident. I trust that most of what you remember will be the joys. But remembrances of dark sorrows will surely be included. Whichever tips the balance, remember you will never know how much you owe to suffering. You may even be surprised at just how little the rich blessings and joy have contributed to your growth in divine life. Be sure, some of the greatest blessings your life will ever know, some of the deepest revelation you will ever peer into, some of the most cherished works the Lord will ever do in your life, yes, the things *you* hold most dear, were but the child of your greatest sorrows!

One day you will make a chance remark to another believer (perhaps one even younger than you are), and be very surprised to discover that your remark deeply blesses and enriches his life. On another occasion, with another Christian whose heart is about to break, you will share something that will change his night to day. You will pause, wonder, and then remember where it was you found that word of wisdom, that oil of comfort.

If you could trace the source, you would find that virtually every help you have ever received—whether it has been from the hands of some brother, or some word in Christian literature, or perhaps from the Scripture—was passed on to you from out of sorrow's fiery furnace and from beneath the bludgeoning blows of suffering's hammer.

Sorrow does have its compensation.

> We comfort others
> With the comfort
> That came to us
> From . . .

* * * * *

Imagine an aged Paul in a dungeon in Rome talking to a people in a city hundreds of miles away. He is addressing a church he has not seen in years, and this is what he tells them:

> You are rejoicing and filled with praise.
> You are doing well in Colossae. Why?
> Because I, Paul, here in Rome, am taking
>   suffering which was actually meant for you.
> I am taking that suffering into my very own body,
>   and that has freed you.
> You are not suffering;
> You are rejoicing.
> The pain destined for you lies here in Rome
>   and is now in my body.

Suffering meant for believers in Colossae was being absorbed in Rome by Paul. He agonized while they gloried.

But even *these* are not the last of his mind-boggling words. He pressed on to say, "For *this* I was made a minister."

Paul saw himself as one who was to take up part of the sufferings that really belonged to the church. For *this* purpose—this *incredible* purpose—he was made a minister. You know, Chris, you really shouldn't hope to be a worker. But if you become a worker, remember the words of that man there in that forsaken cell and make them your own: "To suffer for the church, to suffer *in her place*, for this I was made a minister!"

On some future occasion when things are really getting rough you might remember those words.

Keep reminding yourself of this, "For *this* I was made a minister."

I need to be reminded, too.

* * * * *

Look carefully at Paul's comments on this subject for there is even more.

> Now I rejoice in my sufferings.
> They are for your sake.
> In my body
> I am doing my part
> For His body
> To complete
> What is not finished
> Of Christ's afflictions.

Christ did not finish His sufferings while here on earth? There is more suffering for Him to complete? Is this what Paul is telling us? And is he saying that he, Paul, could complete those sufferings? Or at least play a part in seeing that those sufferings are completed? The mind drowns in the idea.

Jesus Christ did not complete His earthly sufferings—incredible! Especially after all He went through. He was called "illegitimate." What shame this cast upon Him and His mother. He was rejected by friends, family, disciples, and eventually by all mankind. Now to feel rejected is a terrible thing, and He experienced the full brunt of that experience. He was misunderstood; He was misquoted. He felt the cold, cruel stings of burning hate. He wept over man, over sin, over Jerusalem. Twelve men broke His heart.

And beyond all that, Gethsemane and the cross. Was not that enough?

To understand this enigma, we have to see something of *the mystery*. And that mystery was so real to Paul that he could make this statement to Colossian Christians, and make it without commentary.

The Lord did not complete His suffering.

Chris, get a good hold on this: It has been given to the church to complete the sufferings of Christ. Suffering not yet filled up waits out there for you.

But were they not Christ's sufferings? Yes. Then is it not for Christ to go through those sufferings? Yes.

But now we must ask a question: "Which *part* of Christ shall know that suffering?"

Here we come to the unfathomable mystery. It is the mystery of oneness. There is Christ who is the Head . . . that is, He who lived upon the earth, who was crucified, rose, and ascended and now reigns. But there is another part of Christ. There is a part of Christ that is right here, right now, upon the earth today—visible— portraying Christ daily before the entire world. I speak of the physical, visible body of Christ. You see, the body is also Christ. The body, which is the church, is part of that Christ. There is suffering out there yet to be endured, yet to be known, yet to be embraced by that part of Christ which is called the body.

We all thank God that no one member of that body will ever have to know and endure all the sufferings that Jesus Christ experienced while living on earth. But each one of us—because we are in some mysterious way one with Him—will taste some part of His experience of suffering.

One within your fellowship may know *ridicule*. Another will partake of *physical* pain, another will know *rejection*; perhaps someone else may taste what it means to be *vilified* and verbally, socially crucified. And perhaps, just perhaps, there will be one within your fellowship who will touch that awful thing which Christ touched in that last moment of the cross: the dark night of the spirit.

There is one aspect of the cross that none of us will ever know—praise God! We will never know what it means to be the sin-bearer. That is one thing which I will never experience, nor will you. He and He alone has experienced that. He experienced the one thing that none of us should have escaped, and the one thing which He need never have known. He became the sin-bearer and thereby took suffering that was truly mine.

Now you must step into your place in the body of Christ, and you must receive and you must bear some segment of the suffering which is Christ's—that is, that part of Christ which is the church.

> If you ever see a great work of God,
> Something joyous,
> Alive and real,
> Something of Christ,
> Something that *is* Christ,
> Something enduring,
> Then you can be certain of one thing;
> Some lonely saint
> Silent, alone
> Went to the cross
> Suffered, died
> And fell into the earth.
>
> And for what did he die?
> For that lovely harvest,
> That work of God

Which you now see
And declare to be so beautiful.

There must be another day,
And another body of believers.
A day when someone else
Must fall into the earth
And die.
That someone may need be you.

What happened to Paul there in Colossae first
happened to Jesus Christ while on the earth. Next, it
will be your turn.

You *will* be suffering.

How long?

Throughout your whole sojourn upon this planet!

"But," you say, "each year He applies His cross to
me more and more."

Yes, and each of us is being filled up to full measure
by the suffering of Christ. He is doing that in me, in
you. That little assembled group where you gather will
at last touch the sufferings of Christ. Filling up—on
your part—His sufferings.

You will not know all of His sufferings, nor will you
know all of *your* portion of His sufferings at once. His
suffering will be scattered about throughout your whole
pilgrimage. Remember that you, one small member of
His body, will not, cannot, know all His suffering. But
what of you *and* the others there in the assembly of
saints where you meet? Yes! There, you can. There,
you should. There, you *must*.

Together you are to fill up, bring to completion, the
sufferings of Christ. This is one of your destinies as a
body of people gathering in His name.

What God accomplished in His Son in Judea He is

now seeking fully to accomplish in the body. She is to know, she is to experience, she is to enter into His suffering, and you shall have some part in this great drama.

* * * * *

Simon Peter stretched our understanding of suffering in a line he once penned in a letter.

> Let your rejoicing come forth
> According to how much the measure of
> Your suffering matches the suffering of Christ.

If you suffer a little, rejoice a little. If your suffering begins to take on immensity, the immensity of Christ's own suffering, then rejoice even more. And if you should touch His Gethsemane, if you should touch His last hour on the cross, then, dear saint of God, lift your rejoicing to the skies!

What a mountain! What a view!

My, those brothers of Century One had such an incredible view of suffering. Sometimes I look into the haunted eyes of a dear brother or sister and see them on the very edge of sanity and wonder what would happen if I told them, at that moment, to do what Peter has told them they are to do. Surely that ancient brother was standing on a mountain most of us simply have not yet found. He was seeing things which our eyes have not yet opened to.

When you sense that some negative, uncomfortable or downright painful thing has fallen into your life, you have several choices. You can do what all of us usually do—lament, mourn, get depressed, go into self-pity. You might also try rejoicing, but it's a rare saint that successfully does that. In fact, most of us want to break out in red hives when we see someone suffering greatly and rejoicing in Christ. We wonder how they do that.

When suffering comes your way, there is one thing that you certainly will do: You will ask the Lord, "*Why* has this happened?" Chris, there is something else almost as certain.

You will receive no answer.

If the "why" could be removed, dear brother, most of the transforming power of the cross would disappear. The "why" factor of the cross is perhaps its sharpest, most effective, most deadly aspect. Remove the "why" factor of the cross and there really isn't much suffering involved in it.

Then why are you suffering? It is impossible for me, or for anyone else, to answer with certainty. But of this you can be sure; you are fellowshipping in the sufferings of Christ. Your suffering is no greater than His, and the great things which suffering accomplished in His life are now working in you to produce some of those same great accomplishments.

* * * * *

If you cannot *cherish* what it is the Lord is doing in your life, at least do not *waste* what He is doing in your life. Lay down the self-pity, and with all the strength and grace that He allows you, yield to His work. If you cannot make it up within you to yield totally to your Gethsemane (most of us can't), then at least yield up to light the dark feelings of resentment and bitterness that are trying to hatch inside you.

One day you are going to come to the conclusion that serving the Lord is mostly crying . . . and suffering . . . and agonizing. What can you do in that sad hour? Nothing really, except bend over double and absorb into your being those sufferings, sufferings which really belong to the church. In that hour, bear her sufferings for her.

And if you happen to look up, you will see her going on her way, gloriously rejoicing. She will be oblivious to the fact that she is, at that moment, so very glorious because you have suffered.

* * * * *

The trial you are going through is cutting away *something!* Whatever it is, the thing cut out will be replaced by something that is immeasurably glorious.

Oh, the lengths He goes to to teach us tenderness, compassion, and . . . well . . . just the simple "how to" of loving another brother or sister. I have watched Christians come into the fellowship of the body of Christ at age 21 and then beheld them again ten years later. Surprisingly, even in the best possible environment, they look very much the same. There is, in fact, the same personality and the same basic dispostion; nonetheless, there is a difference. The young Christian college student who walked in here ten years ago to gather with a group of other believers sitting on the floor of a large living room was a Christian capable of hurting others so deeply and being so insensitive in the doing of it. The person who sits here in that same room today is now very quick to cry, very slow to correct, very good at comforting and encouraging others, very poor at passing judgment and finding fault.

Do you think it was the books he read? Do you think it was the messages she heard? No. It was the chilly nights of the spirit that brought this change.

Chapter 34

Dear Chris:

What is the Lord doing in your life through suffering? No matter how certain you are that you know, the truth is, you are not certain. One day the reason for your present suffering will be revealed. I do not mean by that, it will be made known to *you*; I mean it will be revealed just as an exquisite masterpiece is revealed before an expectant audience. One day the master work that He is doing within you will be revealed before angels, before principalities and powers, before men, before all created things.

What is that masterpiece? Nothing less than the Bride of Christ, His very wife. Think about her for a moment: a girl as glorious as He is glorious. One day she will be revealed, a human being, transformed: yes, *divinely* transformed up to the measure where she can be the wife of the one who is the eternal Son of the living God.

* * * * *

Jesus Christ came into this world a bachelor. He also came here as the only one of His species, the divine race. He came here with no mate: behold the *only* species that had no "she." Adam had a mate; the animals had mates; but God was without a mate. Eve matched Adam, for she was the female version of a human being. But there was no female version of God.

He wished to obtain that very thing: a girl, a bride, for Himself.

He knew He could not accomplish this feat without there being an infinite amount of suffering involved. And that suffering came, first, to the Godhead! Secondly that suffering had to come to that *girl*. He was the pathfinder of pain and suffering. She only follows in His steps. If that girl is ever to stand beside Him as His bride, if she is to be qualified to rule with Him, she must also suffer. If she is to be *one* with Him in all other things, that is, the *glorious* things of being His bride, then it follows that she must be one with Him in suffering.

Because you, Chris, are part of that bride—the church—you must, and you will, enter into her sufferings. Her sufferings, in turn, are but His suffering. Her sufferings are nothing more than her entering into the sufferings of the Godhead.

Suffering is inherited, not only in the ways of God, but in the very being of God. He accepted that fact and then moved down the road of His own experience into pain and sorrow. Chris, accept that fact, and move on down the same road.

Remember,

> This light affliction
> Is not to be compared
> With the glory
> Set before you.

What is that glory? I don't know. Not fully. But I know one aspect of that glory. Ask any girl who is desperately in love with a boy and who is betrothed to marry him. Better, ask a commoner who is about to wed a great king. There is at least part of her glory.

While the Lord Jesus lived upon this earth, He offered up many prayers and supplication, with much crying and tears. He offered those prayers up to a Father who had the power to save Him from death. But it was the Father's will that He die. My, what a view God has of suffering. He allowed it in His own Son. No, He decreed it! Now the Son, despite the fact He was the only Son of God, had to work His way through a process of *learning* . . . learning obedience to *that* will. And He did learn obedience. How did He learn it? *By the things which He suffered.* Suffering was the school master, the teacher, of Jesus Christ.

The subject matter?

Obedience to God.

How will *you* learn obedience to that same God?

Shall she have a history different from His?

* * * * *

If you would complain, remember that long before creation, something awful, even horrible, had happened to the Godhead. Before He created eternity, before He created angels, or the heavens, or earth, or anything . . . He had already suffered more than any of us will ever suffer. He knew in advance how necessary suffering would be to the scheme of things. He knew He would suffer, and He knew just *how much* suffering we would suffer. He knew *based on His own personal experience of it before creation!* The Godhead accepted the fact that there would be the certainty of suffering in our universe . . . for Himself and for the most precious thing in the universe to Him . . . His wife. He knew, yet He was not turned back by that experiential knowledge. He calculated the enormity of the suffering, beheld the end result and decided it was all worth it! If any man questions that decision, that man should pause and remember just what experience of suffering Jesus Christ had in His life upon which He based His decision.

I was slain
Before the foundation
Of the world.

* * * * *

Jesus Christ loves that girl whom we call the church. He loves her far beyond anything we fallen creatures, trapped as we are here in the corridor of time, can ever understand. And she loves Him. She has proven that love again and again through the centuries, but she will yet love Him more. She will love Him with more abandon and more passion than we can now grasp. But understand, there can be no such mutual abandonment, no such self-giving of love, without suffering. There is no love without self-giving, and there is no self-giving without sorrow in our lives.

Even the Lord Jesus could not come up to the full mark of abandoned love without having drunk the cup of suffering. Think what the Father did when He gave His Son to die. He was provoked by love. And out of the pain of that experience, His love grew. He loves her more now. And as she drinks of His cup, she learns that the heights of love are not reached except by suffering. There is something about suffering that rips aside that which is not divine and leaves a divine interchange of love, not self, at the center of all things.

It is the Father's desire that the Bride of Christ be as nearly like the Son as the Son is like the Father. (Do you know just how much the Son *is* like the Father?) If this is to take place, then a great deal which is *not* part of the divine nature that is in us . . . well, that part *must* be dealt with. Some things must be *dealt* with, other things *broken*, yet other things *transformed* and perhaps a little must be *consumed*. That part of you that *is* the divine nature must grow and be enhanced. This is the Lord's way in the universe. The quality the Son desires in the Bride is no less than the quality the Father has in His Son. Some of the quality will be gained by the Bride at the end of the ages, but some of it must be gained here.

* * * * *

He has two methods for accomplishing transformation. First, there is His very own life growing within you: pulsating, ever expanding, swallowing up. How glorious!

And He has the cross. The cross cuts away, making room, so that *His* life might continue to grow outward from the center.

You will enjoy the first part, the growth of the divine nature within you! But oh! How you will reel under the working of the cross as it makes room for that growth!

Taking away the dark side of your humanity until nothing remains but (1) the divinity you received into you on the day of your conversion and (2) a *transformed* humanity. . .this is His goal.

Progress is being made, Chris! Yes, even though sometimes progress is *retreat*! And when will He be finished? He will not quit in you until that last breath is heaved or until that day when He returns. Until then, *He* works.

And what is the ultimate purpose of all these things?

> For it is by Him,
> For it is through Him,
> For it is to Him
> All things are created,
> Visible and invisible,
> Things in other realms,
> Things in our realm,
> By Him,
> For Him,
> To Him.

He came before everything that ever happened. And everything that is happening makes sense through Him.

Most of all remember, *He* is head of the church, which is His body. And *you* are a member of her, and whatever happens to you, it is by Him, it is through Him, it is for Him, and one day it will be to Him. The final glory shall be His.

I repeat, whatever He is doing to you and through you and for you and by you today, in the church, is for Him and to Him and through Him and by Him.

Let's change that a little. For she is by Him, she is through Him, and she is for Him . . . and one day she shall be one with Him in glory. Your Lord will go to any lengths to prepare for Himself a bride.

All divine activity in this universe revolves around

the church of Jesus Christ. All that is deposited in that church is ultimately for Him.

Part IV

Chapter 35

It was John of the Cross, writing four centuries ago, who made famous the term, *"Dark night of the soul."* We might more accurately refer to this experience as a "dark night of the spirit." This term speaks of a time in a believer's life when the presence of the Lord *seems* to have totally disappeared.

What exactly is this unusual experience? How can it be correctly identified?

It is easier to explain what the experience is *not* than what it is. A dark night of the spirit is not a dry spell, nor is it "having a hard time." It certainly is not what almost all of us say some time in our lives, "I just don't feel the Lord's presence." Neither is it personal illness, nor is it persecution. We are not referring to being out of a job, nor to a period of confusion, nor to the world and its problems, be they small or great. This is not in reference to a person having psychological problems, nor to the psychotic. Oddly, it is not a sense that *you* have forsaken the Lord; perhaps—strictly speaking—not even that He has forsaken you.

Then what is this experience, this suffering? Our best understanding of this experience can be grasped by beholding it as it was known in the life of the Son of God.

Why bother to look at this experience, or even acknowledge its existence?

Because it helps us to understand our Lord and how He works. Sometimes, by looking at the worst of things and the principles involved in them, we come to better understand the smaller ways of God in our everyday life.

Chapter 36

There in the Judgment Hall He stood, being hated. He heard an endless string of lies being spoken against Him. Earlier He had felt His body ripped apart. His face and head had been deliberately mutilated. Even without the awaiting cross He might have died of the physical abuse already inflicted upon Him.

It is a tragic scene...often told, often considered, a study in human injustice. Yet the events of the Judgment Hall pale when compared to those which later transpired upon the cross. What is *not* frequently considered is that all other aspects of the cross pale in comparison to the seconds just before He died.

As a believer it is given you to enter, in some small way, into a portion of the cross of Jesus Christ. *That* is a very sobering consideration, is it not? But as you consider the cross, add this: Something worse than the cross looms out there. At least, there is one portion of the cross unlike anything else. Something transpired in that last, bitter moment of the cross which neither human lips can describe nor human soul identify. Little can be said in the discussions of it; even less comfort can be extended to that pilgrim who might be called upon to taste of it.

> My God, My God
> Why! Why Hast *Thou*
> Forsaken ME?!

Something He embraced out there, some dreadful experience He went through, some dark, hell-like thing He encountered in the corridors of His inner person was inexplicable, utterly indescribable and horrible in the extreme. A horror so vast that the Son of God broke under the bludgeonings of its inward invasion.

Because we Christians encounter no spiritual experiences except those which our Lord has first tasted and because we fellowship in His sufferings, then it follows that some believers among us may also taste that same experience.

Some of our experiences in Christ are glorious experiences, like visitations to other realms; yet they are nothing more than small duplicates of His own. But some of the experiences we have, also small duplicates of His own, seem not so blessed.

A few believers who may be in a practical expression of the body of Christ with you may one day be called on to enter into some small identification with that last moment of the cross.

What is this experience, this thing referred to as "a dark night"? Allow me, for the sake of communication, to state it in an inaccurate extreme. In that place which is the deepest, most inward part of the believer, something none of us are prepared for *happens*! God removes His indwelling Spirit. The Christian is lost. There is no God within him. There is little evidence of God without. God walks off.

At least this is what *appears* to happen. And, in this case, the appearance is as effective as the fact. For all temporal purposes, a divine departure might as well have taken place.

Then what has actually taken place?

The Christian discovers that he no longer has any

internal sense of the presence of his Lord. It is as though God had extracted Himself from the universe. By all measurable evidence, the Lord has withdrawn from the believer's heart, his soul, his spirit, even from the cells of his body. God is utterly gone. The emptiness itself is an overwhelming thing. Furthermore, as far as the Christian can discern, the Lord has not only departed, but He has done so with finality. It is a forever thing.*

Certainly such an environment does not cultivate hope. It was this hopeless darkness of the spirit that Jesus Christ was going through in the instant of His death. It was not the experience which He *passed through*, but the experience He was in at the moment of His death. There is a vast difference between passing through a dark night and dying in the very midst of it.

He died outside hope's warm domain.

Consider that when the cross did its final work—the putting to death of the Son of God—that your Lord died outside of any sense of His Father's presence. He died in *that* state. He had no spiritual sense whatsoever. (Unless we say that the sudden, unexpected, inexplicable act of being forsaken can be classified as a spiritual sense.)

Jesus Christ died in the very midst of "Question's" mazed domain. He died in the vortex of forsakenness.

If you wish to know if a thing you are going through is truly the cross, look for this imprint: when Jesus Christ died He died not knowing what it was the cross was doing to Him. Unless there is a question—a question that receives no answer—there really isn't much of the

---

* I remind the reader, this is an extremely rare experience, known by few, reported by even fewer.

cross involved. The unanswered is perhaps the central characteristic of the cross; it is part of the very molecular structure of the cross. That aspect of the cross, the question, the lack of an answer, is bequeathed to every child of God. Expect it!

You who get so upset with your God when He momentarily leaves you in the small lurches of life, it is true that the riches of your inheritance in Christ are vast and rich, but His ability to forsake you is also within the bounds of your inheritance.

You may sit in the impractical walls of some stained glass cathedral and hear a simplistic, sentimental, shallow sermon on the faithfulness of God and come away seeing Him somewhat as a warm puppy who will never leave you or forsake you. But that is an imaginary god, erected on a very thin piece of ice. The faithfulness of God has been vastly overrated, and His determination to transform—even to the point of implementing *abandonment*—has been forgotten.

Forever let it be recalled: your Lord died abandoned and forsaken. It was not at some unimportant juncture in His life. No, He was abandoned in that moment when we hope, above all other moments, that God will be near. He was abandoned at the moment He was dying! The awful moment of Jesus Christ's greatest doubt, the awful moment of His greatest need to know, and the awful moment of dying—these three intersected His life at the same time. And it was that moment God chose to walk off. What timing! In that moment, Jesus Christ, God's Son, found, not help, not comfort, but the unfaithfulness of God!

He died in a swarm of wonder. He died without one word of solace, reassurance or hope. He died with a view of God's receding back.

Moreover, your Lord died unsure He was going to rise from the dead. Who knows, perhaps He even died fairly certain He would *not* rise from the dead. His Father *had* left Him, you know. Yes, He knew beforehand that He would die. But did He know His own Father would, in the last instant, reject and abandon Him? Just a moment before He died, His whole being had been shattered by His becoming the incarnation of sin. This was followed by the loss of His Father's presence, causing His to call out a question bathed in doubt. No answer came, either within the hearing of His inward spirit or His outward ear. The silence strengthened the doubt.

First forsaken. Then ignored! Then, in that moment of heaven's silence and earth's hatred, with a soul that had become sin, and with His own spirit gasping its last dying breath...then Death came and conquered Him! Consider, you who are followers of this One who is the Christ, consider what it was your God did to Him! Consider and be warned: this same experience has also touched the lives of some of His most devout and deepest followers. Just exactly how loving is your God, anyway? You who take His faithfulness so glibly and expect it so certainly, answer for yourselves. On the basis of the evidence present, just how much can you expect from His faithfulness? Just how trustable is He?

* * * * *

Did I forget something?

Yes, I failed to mention what else happened that weekend. On Friday Jesus Christ was forsaken. The jury went out on Friday. The verdict? Obviously, the grace of God is *not* sufficient. And don't ever forget that stunning fact.

"Surely," you protest, "you must not say that. Look what happened next." Ah! But speaking of what happened next is no more than sermonizing! There is false comfort in future facts when you are *still* living out Friday. Or Saturday, for that matter.

A devout and pious saint who has totally lost all sense of the presence of Christ—when after months or *years* that presence has never returned—*tell him* about the rest of that weekend! At best, your words will be but faint hope.

True, there is something beyond Friday's loss, but on Friday no one knew that! Nor on Saturday. Friday and Saturday deserve more attention. The distance from Friday night to Sunday morning can stretch for years . . . no, forever!

Chapter 37

Of what benefit is it to be a Christian and go through a dark night of the spirit?

Perhaps none! For the moment, let us even assume just that . . . none whatsoever! But you have asked the wrong question. The question should be: "Of what benefit is this 'dark night' experience, not for the Christian, but for the body of Christ?" Ah, now there is a question that sheds light on this mysterious matter.

Do you realize this rather awesome fact: that the church, a girl, was born out of that Friday? The cross was her progenitor. The cross *produced* her! She was born out of Friday's sufferings. She is inseparably linked to that cross. The history of that cross and the history of that girl must forever intertwine. They are of the same molecular structure. That means she will know that cross just as did her Lord.* Included in that, she will know the contents of that last moment of the cross—the Father abandoning the Son. The "dark night" is there. She must, in some small way, be able to at least identify with that experience. And if not she, then at least some member of her body must know.

Today the expression of the church is shallow, old, and traditional. So much about her early ways needs to be restored. How can that first century glory be

---

* No, she will never know one aspect of the cross: that of being sin bearer. By the very nature of redemption, He alone will know that portion of the cross.

rekindled in our day? The answer lies in seeing restored those elements which went together to produce her in the first place. Central to her birth was suffering. And at the center of that suffering lies the dark night of the spirit, experienced by her Lord. Now within her confines, some must touch this same night . . . for the sake of others in the body of Christ.

The church is always born out of suffering, born in the midst of suffering, born as a result of suffering. So was her birth then; so shall be any restoration now.

We are speaking of principles written within her nature. When you remember the garden tomb where she was born, please also pause and remember the experience that immediately preceded that glorious resurrection. The experience of the cross, including a dark night of the spirit, played a part in her birth that was no less central than the resurrection itself!

Resurrection *and* the cross. Those men and women who today dare to gather together for the purpose of seeing the church reach greater heights—to see restoration—will have to be men and women who know the height, the depth, the length and breadth of the reality of all that those two words encompass.

I recommend, before *you* venture too far out in this business of committing yourself to Christ, before you begin finding out the true meaning of the cross and the resurrection. . .surely before you dare the waters of the restoration of church life. . .I solemnly recommend that you recall your Lord's final moments on the cross. Having done so, is it not true that you might more wisely stay home?

No wonder most of us Christians, in expressing the highest limits of our devotion to Christ, do no more than report into a large auditorium for one hour on Sunday morning. Who could blame any of us if we did not become more involved than we do with a God whose ways may include a cross like unto the cross of His Son? Be careful before you abandon your life to Him. And remember, if you meet with Christians in an experience of body life, each of you *will be called on* to enter into at least some small portion of your Lord's suffering. That is a *guaranteed* fact! But why is it a fact? Why must we? The answer is simple. It is for the sake of those around you, for the sake of others within the body.

Written into the very nature of church life is a dark night of the spirit.

Dare *you* then walk this way?

Chapter 38

I heard a simple story in my youth that remains until this day one of my favorites. It seems a black minister of the Civil War days was preaching to his congregation on Easter Sunday morning. Vividly he described the crucifixion and the death of Christ. Then he described how Satan and all the demons of hell rejoiced on the tombstone of the Son of God. At that moment the old minister turned and addressed Lucifer personally.

"You just go ahead and have your fun, but watch out devil, 'cause yonder comes Sunday morning!"

There may be years between Friday and Sunday. The believer may have long ago forgotten there was such a thing as Sunday. Long, long ago it may have been that the Christian settled the matter: "God walked off from me and He shall not return." The matter is not only settled, but with the long passing of time even the concept that He might return has been forgotten. But God cannot forget. Sunday is part of the very nature of God and God cannot deny Himself.

I know of no believer who has ever reported a dark night of the spirit but what he lived long enough, perhaps to his own surprise, to report a bright morning of resurrection.

That forsaken and weary Christian who gave up all hope of ever getting back a functioning spirit over-looked something in the nature and experience of his Lord. Jesus Christ was not forever forsaken. Yes, His Father did walk off. True, God's grace really isn't sufficient. Even the Lord Jesus could testify to that incontestable fact. But Jesus Christ also knows what it is like (far beyond any reasonable lapse of time) to be raised from the dead—suddenly, surprisingly, raised again to life. Yes, He knows what it is like to be jolted back to life again, totally, unexpectedly. His inward being was also resurrected. Blazing. Alive.

One day this very Lord who knows, who truly knows, the full horror of being forsaken, *this* Lord walks by and rattles the tomb of a devout Christian held in the icy grip of a dark night of the spirit. He comes! He comes and sets ablaze those cold and still inward parts of the believer. The dark night of his spirit passes in a burst of returned glory. The indwelling Christ is back in business. And suddenly the Christian knows, truly beyond all mortal bounds of understanding: He *never* forsakes.

"I can't believe it. I was *not* forsaken!"

His grace, oh, His grace *is* sufficient. Late, beyond all comprehension. But sufficient. And in some inexplicable and glorious way . . . right on time.

* * * * *

As the days of his spiritual restoration unfold, this believer begins to learn a good many things about the ways of His God which he never knew before.

He looks back to realize that every moment of those long and lonely months of his dark night were laced with sadness. Every waking moment of his life was dominated by that whelming sense of internal emptiness. Now he begins to recognize just how powerful was that ever-present feeling of nothingness and that endless sense of sadness. Never before in his life, never after, would any internal sense ever be as strong, as constant, as ever conscious, as was that void. Then, in wonder he makes his discovery. That nothingness, that hounding sense of the Lord's absence, was in fact the Lord Himself! As long as he lives he will never have an internal sense *that* strong. He realizes that very absence of a sense of God was overwhelming. Prevailing. Constant! And nothing he will ever experience will ever so constantly, unrelentingly, remind him of Christ.

In darkness that Christian has walked in the ever-present void which also was Christ.

> For to *Him*
> Even the darkness
> Is Light!

Truly, Christian, He *never* leaves us nor forsakes us.

Chapter 39

Earlier we asked the question, "Of what value is a dark night of the spirit?" The answer to that is known only to God. At best, we can only observe. I submit a few possibilities.

Within a practical experience of the body of Christ, it does no harm to have at least one member who cannot be blown out of the water, no matter how pitched the battle. Only faith which has been firmly tempered by suffering and grounded in sorrow can endure the conflict that lies ahead for any group of Christians experiencing church life.

Morever, it is an established spiritual fact that no Christian can be destroyed by circumstances smaller in size and strength than circumstances which he has already survived. And rest assured, it is very difficult to find anything to throw at a Christian which is greater than a dark night of the spirit. If he has survived that, he just might survive most of the other things which the church will be called on to face.

The point is obvious. It is sometimes quite beneficial to the body of Christ to have someone present who has previously survived a devastation even greater than the catastrophe at hand! Do you see that a disaster such as a dark night of the spirit is often the mother of inward peace, and strong faith, and a church's sure foundation in an overwhelming flood of adversity?

Are there other positive things to be said of a dark

night of the spirit? Yes. It is good to have someone in the church who is familiar with a genuine case of resurrection. ("I personally witnessed a resurrection!")

Another possible fruit to come out of a dark night has to do with a deeper, more accurate understanding of a person's internal makeup. For a Christian to be denied the spirit's functionings within him is to have an opportunity to learn well just what parts inside of him are not his spirit but are, rather, the *feelings* of his soul, the *rationale* of the soul's mind, and the *volition* of the soul's will. Then to have the intuitive sense of the spirit return is a strong foundation upon which to begin to truly discern spirit from soul. A more exacting comparison of soul and spirit becomes possible. One can tell what has been added that wasn't there before. Surely we can say that here is something needed by any people gathered in His name: to discern what is soul and what is spirit. Soul and spirit are so intertwined, so similar in many ways, yet utterly different in many other ways. Surely one of the major reasons He sends suffering into our lives is to reach those inward parts and cause us to learn a healthy differentiation between the two.

What more can be said of a dark night? It is one of the greatest tools which your Lord (infrequently) employs for the purpose of crushing soul's strength and making room for spirit's upward growth.

And is there more? Yes, much more. But let this be our final comment. A dark night of the spirit is but one more of the possible privileges which He extends to us all in allowing us to fellowship in the sufferings of Christ, for the sake of the body.

Most of us will never know a dark night of the spirit.

Perhaps no one who ever reads this book will. But to come to some small acquaintance with it is to enlarge our understanding of the cross, of suffering, of transformation . . . and why He works and how He works in us.

Part V

Chapter 40

Chris stared out of his dorm window, watching the distant lightning dance against the backdrop of approaching thunderclouds. As he began following the lazy downward drifts of the first drops of rain upon his window, he heard the crack of a nearby lightning bolt, followed hard by a thunder clap. With it, every light in the dorm went out. Instinctively, Chris turned to face his darkened room. For an instant the electrical storm outside provided his room with a small, intermittent light. Then, suddenly, everything around him went pitch black; and because that was simply impossible, Chris knew immediately what was taking place. For a long time he stood motionless, finally breaking the unearthly spell with one inquiring word:

"Messenger?"

From behind him, and perhaps just a little to his right, Chris heard that disconcertingly calm voice of Messenger.

"Do *not* turn around, young Christian."

Messenger's words were an unmistakable command, and accompanying them came an enormous burst of light breaking over Chris' shoulder. He had the disquietening feeling that should he dare turn he would find the heels of his tennis shoes precariously balanced on the edge of an abyss. Just as that unwelcome idea was settling into his mind Chris felt the strong, reassuring hand of Messenger clasp his arm.

"Now begin to turn around, very slowly. What you are about to see is *time* and *space* in a visible panorama. Do *not* be afraid. As I told you once before, I doubt that you will fall."

For several good reasons, one being that by now there was absolutely nothing under his feet, these words were far less assuring to Chris than on the first occasion he heard them.

As Chris began cautiously to turn, he was certain he would see something which would completely unhinge him. He resisted the urge to cover his eyes, extreme heights not being one of his strong points.

What Chris and Messenger saw was a vast tunnel. The two of them were suspended somewhere near its center, and Chris could tell that the whole thing was slowly turning. Looking down, much as he might from an airplane, he could also see that this green and meadowed tunnel was moving past him. As he looked intently in all directions, Chris saw a thousand scenes from history displayed on the surface of the cylinder. Slowly he began to realize that he was watching the entire drama of humanity, exhibited like some vast kaleidoscope around him.

"I can see . . . I . . . I can see everything. Why, I can *see* time!"

That portion of the tunnel still in front of him seemed to stretch on and on into infinity, while by looking directly beneath him, Chris could see, unmistakably, Jerusalem. Upward and to his right was Rome. Forward and above him were medieval cities. To his left and at a further distance, the glory that was France. In the far, far distance, a modern-day metropolis. Beyond that he was not sure, as everything seemed to converge at some far off point that was wholly obscured in glistening light.

All around, above and beneath him, passed the whole panorama of history. "A living, infinite stage," he whispered.

The only thing that kept Chris from fainting dead away was the sobering thought that should he faint, he might also fall.

"At this moment, in *this* place where you now stand, we are at the very juncture of two creations. There, directly beneath you . . ." Messenger paused.

Chris looked down, almost between his feet. Without question, he could clearly see Golgatha!

"There . . . is the cursed place . . . it is there where, in the eyes of God, all things of His creation were done away. But look, just beyond the cross. See. An empty tomb. *Do you see*, Christian?"

"I see, I see," cried Chris, forgetting his fears in the ecstasy of his discovery.

"It is there that the first element of a *new* creation began!"

"What? What do you mean? What is it? *What* new creation?" asked Chris in an unnecessarily loud voice.

Messenger turned and stared at Chris, a look of incredulity upon his face.

"You mean that you do not know?" replied Messenger in quiet unbelief. "Will your species never learn its riches? *You* ask *me* what new creation? This new creation," he said, pointing directly at Chris. "*Christians*, that's what! The sons and daughters of God, born out of the womb of the empty tomb, the church... YOU!

"Do you not know that in His rising from the dead,

He brought you forth as the first fruits of a new creation? Christian, *you* are a new creation—created *in* Christ Jesus our Lord!''

As his mind reeled from the things he had seen, as well as at his own ignorance, Chris lost his balance, stumbling.

Quickly Messenger thrust out a hand and steadied the young man. Without so much as pausing, he pointed with his other hand to that distant place at the far end of the tunnel. Once again, Chris strained to see just what mystery was hidden behind that brilliant light.

"There," continued Messenger in a voice that contained a slight note of joy, "there is the end of all ages. And the beginning of the *Age of all Ages*."

"Huh?" blurted Christian.

Again, Messenger stared at Christian in bewilderment.

"I speak of the *Consummation of the ages*, the end of all things old, the *beginning* of a new heaven and a new earth."

Messenger paused. Then, in softer but more absent words he said, "The new creation. That for which we all so desperately long!

"Nothing of *this* creation will survive into the new creation. Nothing except, of course, those things which are presently in the old creation but which do not belong to it!"

Chris found himself fighting to suppress another "huh!" and managed to express his ignorance a little more clearly.

"What's in *this* creation but doesn't belong here?"

Messenger sighed. "I just told you. The firstfruits of the new creation. The church."

Rather than compound his confusion, Chris turned his gaze back to the brightness glowing so beautifully out there at time's end.

"Come, Christian," said Messenger addressing a very transfixed young man. "Come, let us visit a few of time's small places. There will be little need of conversation as it will be granted you to understand much of what you are about to see."

Chris felt himself moving forward and downward. Or was it time which was moving past them?

Chapter 41

"Are we in my own time?" asked Christian as he caught sight of what was obviously a college dormitory.

"No, the time is some 33 years before your time."

Chris found himself in a second-floor dormitory room. Sitting at a desk before him was a young man. Chris felt a strange sense come over him. Something was familiar about the young man, or at least something *should* be familiar about him.

"That's Uncle Bill!That's Bill when he was about my age. This is the place where he got saved! This is the day he was born again, isn't it, Messenger! Isn't it?"

Chris was about to grasp Messenger and shake the answer out of him but was stopped short when Messenger raised his hand.

"Look intently at your uncle, Chris. It is important that you see him. No, that you see *into* him. You will see those things which *are* but which belong to the unseen realm."

The room seemed to fade, and along with it the table and chair disappeared. All Chris could see was a young Bill Young, his head bowed, his face resting in his hands. Slowly Bill began also to fade, but as he did, something else began to appear...something inside Bill. The scene held, with Bill's image not completely faded out, the other not quite in clear view. Chris stared intently.

"What is it? What is it I'm seeing inside Bill?"

"Something from another realm."

"What?"

"Look closely."

Chris shifted uncomfortably. Whatever it was, he had some intuitive sense that it was dead. Messenger spoke again, addressing Chris' thoughts. "No, Chris, not totally dead, yet dead."

Once more Chris heard himself saying, "huh?" and wished dreadfully he could stop doing that.

"Dead to the other realm. Dead to the realm from which it came. Yes, dead to the realm of its origin."

"I'm sorry, Messenger, but this time you've lost me completely," confessed Chris.

"A moment ago you spoke of this being the day that Bill was born again. You are correct. This is the day that Bill was born from above; and, if you will step back, you will see exactly what that means."

Chris stepped back, his eyes still fixed on that small *something* which was deep inside Bill. Whatever it was, it mesmerized Chris.

Messenger spoke again. "You are about to see the resurrection—not of the body, but of man's spirit, that portion of his being which died in Adam. You are also about to *see the partaking of the divine nature*. Come Chris, we are about to visit the other realm. We will *see* "being born from above."

Chris caught his breath and locked it in. He was seized with terror. He thought, "Me? In the other realm? I'll never get out of this alive."

"Our visit will be short. You will see very little. Only that which pertains to this room and the young student named Bill, who is about to offer up the first prayer he ever prayed to his Lord, his God and His Savior."

At Messenger's behest, Chris turned around. What he saw above him was a door.

"This is that door of which you have been so curious, young Christian. Beyond that door are realms unseen, where exist neither time nor space. The spiritual. Even the heavenly place . . . that is our destination.

"Notice, please, that the door is above you, Christian. Always, it is *above.*"

Messenger took Chris' trembling hand. Chris felt himself rising. Terror stricken, he closed his eyes and, for one brief moment, regretted that he had ever been born. With that, the two passed from the seen realm into the unseen realm.

Chapter 42

Chris stood facing the door between the two realms, his eyes clamped shut in terror. Messenger, with his two strong hands, was holding him immobile.

"We have just passed through the door that joins our two realms, and you are now standing in *heavenly places*. I have turned you so that you face your own realm, not mine. When you open your eyes, continue to stand exactly where I have placed you or you will endanger your life, for behind you is an infinite realm of light which you were not constructed to survive."

Despite the fact that he was almost paralyzed with fear, Chris cracked open his eyes. Light swarmed around him. His only point of orientation was the open door directly in front of him. Through it, to his amazement, he could still clearly see the figure of a young college student with his head bowed in prayer. Chris was certain that his very existence depended on his ability to focus all attention on that praying student.

Messenger spoke again. "Watch carefully. Listen intently."

Chris strained forward. The form of Bill Young was directly in front and slightly below him. He saw Bill move his head slightly and then heard him whisper,

"Lord."

It was as if that word belonged only to heavenly places, for the sound of it came undiminished through the door. And with its utterance, the distance between the door and Bill Young began to close. Heavenly places, it seemed to Chris, had just moved toward Bill!

Chris caught his breath and locked it in as he realized that something—something awesome—was taking place behind him. Automatically, but foolishly, Chris turned around.

Unimaginable light assaulted his eyes. Yet in the midst of it, at some far distant place, there was an even greater light, and at its core Chris was certain he could see the outline of a . . . throne! At the very center of that throne an awesome drama was unfolding. Chris jerked back; everything in his entire being felt as though it was disintegrating. Whirling, in terror and blindness, he fell toward the door.

Messenger quickly picked Chris up, carefully keeping his face away from the blinding light. "I warned you," came the calm voice. "Tell me, Christian, what was it you saw?"

Dazed, Chris wandered through several incoherent sentences and finally said, "It, it was like . . . a comet, an indescribably brilliant comet . . . being born . . . exploding from out of the center of something, something brighter than a thousand suns. And . . . and as the comet hurled out of that sun . . . it left a trail of light . . . an unbroken trail of light . . . still joining the two together . . . comet *still* united with sun."

With urgency in his voice, Messenger responded, "Well said. Quickly now, the door! You are about to *see* regeneration. You are about to see an 18-year-old Bill Young—*born from above*."

Messenger then turned and faced in the direction of the approaching light, his entire vestige almost disappearing in its reflected glory. Messenger raised one hand and, as he did, every moment seemed to slow—how, exactly, Chris did not know, but he was certain that it was for his own benefit.

By now virtually everything was swallowed up in light, and even the outline of Messenger had disappeared. Only the images of the door and Bill Young just beyond it were discernible. And the door! The door was moving again. Toward Bill. Until it seemed to move right inside him.

Confusion now compounded with wonder in Chris' mind.

"How can it be?" Chris was about to shout. Then he heard Messenger's voice somewhere off to the right of him.

"Remember, Mortal, you are in a realm where there is neither time nor space. Here nothing is large or small. Nor is there physical matter as you understand it. Yes, you have seen the door pass into Bill. The entrance between two worlds is now *in* him. The door rests inside his human spirit. This is not a strange thing to citizens of this realm; the human spirit is a God-breathed thing which long ago had its origin in this realm. In that fair garden of long ago it was placed in man at the moment of his creation.

"The first man, Adam, was a soul. Nonetheless, he received a spirit within his bosom that came from *this* domain. In his disobedience, that spirit died; died, that is, to its place of origin. Now you are about to see a regeneration, even a resurrection, of that spirit within one of the sons of Adam.

Chris felt certain that, if he dared, he could reach out and touch that still, gray thing he saw just in front of him. He might have done just that, except that his attention was drawn away by that ball of light which he had seen plummeting from the throne. He was certain that light was coming toward the door. Once again Chris had to fight with all his will to keep from turning around, but that thought gave way to the realization that—if it was coming in this direction—he was standing in its path!

Laboriously, Chris moved to the left, just as the ball of light began to appear over his right shoulder.

"It's alive!" cried Chris. "Alive! Pure, beyond all description, pulsating, and alive!"

For one brief instant, just as it moved past him, Chris was totally swallowed up in the glow of its brightness. For one microsecond, the only thing Chris could definitely find of himself was his eyes; all else had momentarily been submerged in light.

Slowly, the sphere of *living* light passed by Chris and approached the door's edge. Just before it reached the door, the fore gleam of its radiance passed through the door and touched that cold, gray thing that lay just beyond. Suddenly, there was another burst of light. That "thing" in Bill had been awakened! It, too, was now alive!

Right before Christian's astonished eyes, the human spirit had been made alive, again, to its native realm.

For one brief instant there was light emitting from *both* sides of the door. Then that ball of life and light, which had its origin somewhere within the throne of God, plunged through the door.

Chris felt a sudden and unexpected fear for Bill's life. "That, that light, that life, is going *inside* Bill. He can't possibly survive with *that* in him!"

But on it hurled, leaving behind a trail of unbroken light which, Chris was certain now, reached all the way back to the throne of God! "Perhaps," he found himself muttering, "perhaps even to the very bosom of God!"

"Can Bill survive?" Chris called out, not really expecting an answer.

The ball of living light now plunged through the door. The door, the boundary separating the two realms, everything—seemed to dissolve. For a moment Chris was not sure what had happened. Where was the door? The boundary? It had all vanished. Two realms seemed somehow to have joined within the glow of that burning light. Further, that living sphere of...whatever it was...and the enlivened spirit of Bill Young seemed to have done the same.

Almost incoherently, Chris kept repeating to himself, "That living light, that life, is *in* Bill." Then he recalled something he had recently been memorizing. A verse of Scripture; words belonging to Simon Peter:

> For we
> have become
> partakers
> of the
> divine nature.

Once again Chris had the sense that his very being was about to dissolve if something didn't let up. He felt his knees begin to buckle.

Chris Young fell forward in a dead faint.

Chapter 43

It was the sound of a mockingbird and the smell of newly mown grass that first floated into Christian's emerging consciousness. But with them came no inclination to move or even to think. Chris just lay there caressing the grass beneath his fingers.

As a few coherent thoughts finally managed to surface, he opened his eyes. Messenger stood right in front of him. Chris rolled over and sat up. After some time, he dropped his head and spoke softly, "I've seen enough. I understand. I promise you I'll never doubt again as long as I live, and I'll never, never complain about *anything*."

There was humor in Messenger's voice as he replied, "You still don't understand. You will doubt many times. You will fill the skies with complaints. In fact, I advise you not to promise anything. Since the Fall, I have observed that you mortals have had a difficult time living up to even the smallest of promises.

"Come, we have one more small visit to make ere we complete our little pilgrimage."

"Will I see you again, ever?" asked Christian with hope in his eyes.

"That is a decision which rests in other hands."

"Where do we go from here?"

Messenger gave Christian one of those stares that is a compound of puzzlement and sorely tried patience. "*Here* is where we go!" Messenger declared as he pointed to the place where they stood.

Startled, Chris jumped to his feet and swung around in a full circle. "Great gravy! That's the municipal swimming pool over there. This is the city park in my home town. I used to come out here and play when I was a kid." Then Chris stopped, his legs and hands still spread wide apart. "Messenger, I was... converted in *this* park!"

"I know," said that cool, unnerving voice. "In fact, I would recommend you look in that direction. I fancy you might see someone you know rather well."

"I...I don't believe it!" Christian cried in astonishment.

Chris gripped Messenger by the shoulder and began to shake him. "That's *me* over there. Do you hear? That's me! I don't believe it. I tell you, that's me! *This* is the day I got saved! I don't believe it."

"Believe," said Messenger mildly. "After all, you just told me you would never doubt again."

"May I talk to...uh...*him*?!"

"Oh, you may try if you wish, but he...*you*... will not hear. Besides, do you desire to intrude on a moment of such high import? It is the day you acquired eternal life!"

Chris turned and stared at the young man sitting at a picnic table about 50 meters away. Turning back to Messenger, his whole demeanor changed. Chris asked, almost embarrassed, "I'm only supposed to watch, is that it?"

"Yes. You may go to his side. There you may watch the occurrence of your own salvation as it took place in time and space."

Immediately Chris began traversing the distance between himself and a young lad sitting at a picnic table, intently engrossed in a book. When he was within 10 meters, he was unable to go any farther. A little confused, he turned to Messenger. But Messenger, standing almost at his side, seemed to be fading. Chris could see right through him.

"You're—you're disappearing!"

"As you are—to me," replied Messenger.

"What does it mean?"

"It means our time together is coming to a close. I will shortly be in my realm and you will return to your own time."

"But what about him?" asked Chris, pointing to the nearby youth.

"We will finish our observation here. Turn now and watch *yourself* receive eternal life."

"I'm not sure I can survive going through an experience like that again," said Chris hesitantly.

"Ah, but it is not at all the same when viewed from this realm. Now watch. Can you see inside this young man as you saw inside your uncle?"

"Yes!" cried a startled Chris. "Yes, I can! There's that still, cold, gray thing in him...in *me*! Just like it was in Bill!"

Chris stopped. His countenance dropped. "But it doesn't seem to take up as much space in me as it did in Uncle Bill. It's a lot smaller!"

Chris shifted around to look Messenger full in the face. "Is there something wrong with me? Why is that place in me so small?"

"You are correct, Christian, the human spirit is indeed very small, much smaller than it appeared to you when you saw inside Bill. In truth it cannot be seen at all. I remind you, your *body* has weight and size: height, depth, length and breadth. Your body is matter. Physical. In a word, it has dimension. Even your soul occupies time and space. But your *spirit*, well, although it is a part of your very being, totally yours, yet it is of a realm that is without dimension.

"To be accurate, I cannot even say the human spirit is small; it is neither small nor large. It is native to a realm where such words have no meaning. What you see is something you have been allowed to see...but something which belongs to the unseen and the immeasurable.

"But this I will tell you, Christian. *It can grow!* It is capable of being enlarged. But you will not fully understand these matters within the span of your mortal life. Now turn again. Watch the young man before us. Our time together is quickly running out."

The young man sitting at the concrete table turned a leaf in the book and then closed it. There was a pause, and the youth began to cry.

Chris blurted out, "That's—that's the very moment I turned my life over to Jesus Christ. I know it was. I know it was!"

At that moment, a small, soft glow appeared deep within the inmost part of the young man who was now weeping.

"It's so tiny, Messenger; the light inside is so tiny. Not like in Bill at all. I can hardly see it." Agitated, Chris turned to Messenger again. "What's wrong?"

"Nothing. Nothing at all. What you see before you is the same occurrence that takes place inside all believers. I assure you that this is the same awesome visitation you witnessed in Bill."

"But it was so spectacular the other time," said Chris in growing frustration. "I feel cheated."

"It is always spectacular, Christian, when viewed

from my realm; we who live there behold this sacred thing with awe and joy."

Chris stared at the tiny glow for a long time. His one overwhelming thought was *how much* of him there was which was *not* that small speck of glowing light and life.

Messenger spoke again. "I must leave you now, my friend. What you are seeing is the first evidence of the indwelling Christ. As the years roll on He will slowly—but unrelentingly—work His way outward...touching, changing, and reducing Chris Young more and more. He will work Himself outward by any and all means, both convenient and inconvenient, as you have already discovered in the short time you have known Him. And as He works His way outward, following no predictable rules or methods, He will enlarge His place within *you*.

"Now, young man, as He journeys out to you, you also have a journey to make. An inward journey. It is yours, young Christian, to turn your soul inward—toward Him.

"Now it is time. We must bid one another farewell. It is certain we will meet again at least once more—on the Day of all days. But before we depart, look again at that new Christian. Today he received Eternal Life—the Christ of God. Unwittingly, that young man has been joined to another realm. He has inherited all the riches in heavenly places. Now, if God be merciful, this new Christian will stumble upon those things which will greatly aid him in learning how to begin his *inward journey*."

With that Messenger raised his arms and everything in front of Chris began to dissolve. For one flash of a second he thought he saw the very end of that strange tunnel he had traveled in with Messenger. In it something appeared so quickly neither mind nor eye could register it. What he saw he was not sure. A beautiful, beautiful girl, robed in white? Lovely beyond all description, running toward something or someone? The scene, which he was not even sure really happened, vanished in a coat of blackness.

Chris stood very, very still as he had learned to do in these moments of strange transition. A kind of non-time seemed to pass before him—more, it seemed, than he had been accustomed to on previous occasions.

Chris was becoming just a little uneasy when he saw something flash in the distance. There was a pause, and it happened again, a flashing blue-white light. He struggled to remember where he had seen such things before. Then he heard the roll of thunder. And the sound of soft rain beating against his window.

The Beginning.

Order At Your Bookstore